CliffsNotes™

D070241D

Pride and Prejudice

By Marie Kalil, M.A.

IN THIS BOOK

- Learn about the Life and Background of the Author
- Preview and Introduction to the Novel
- Explore themes, character development, and recurring images in the Critical Commentaries
- Examine in-depth Character Analyses
- Acquire an understanding of the novel with Critical Essays
- Reinforce what you learn with CliffsNotes Review
- Find additional information to further your study in the CliffsNotes Resource Center and online at www.cliffsnotes.com

WILEY

Wiley Publishing, Inc.

About the Author

Marie Kalil received her M.A. from the University of Nebraska-Lincoln, specializing in nineteenth-century British and American literature. She has taught at the University of Nebraska at Omaha and Iowa Western Community College.

Publisher's Acknowledgments

Editorial

Project Editor: Tere Drenth

Acquisitions Editor: Gregory W. Tubach

Glossary Editors: The editors and staff of Webster's New World Dictionaries

Editorial Administrator: Michelle Hacker

Production

Indexer: Johnna VanHoose Dinse

Proofreader: York Production Services, Inc.

Wiley Indianapolis Composition Services

CliffsNotes™ Austen's *Pride and Prejudice*

Published by:

Wiley Publishing, Inc.

111 River Street

Hoboken, NJ 07030

www.wiley.com

Copyright © 2000 Wiley Publishing, Inc., New York, New York

ISBN: 0-7645-8607-6

Printed in the United States of America

20 19 18 17 16 15 14 13 12 11

1O/RV/RQ/QT/IN

Published by Wiley Publishing, Inc., New York, NY

Published simultaneously in Canada

Library of Congress Cataloging-in-Publication Data

Kalil, Marie.
   CliffsNotes Pride and Prejudice/ by Marie Kalil.
      p.   cm.
   Includes bibliographical reference and index.
   ISBN 0-7645-8607-6 (alk. paper)
   1. Austen, Jane, 1775-1817. Pride and Preju-
dice--Examinations--Study guides. I. Title: Pride
and Prejudice. II. title.
PR4034.P72 K35 2000
823'.7--dc21   00-038058
                                                            CIP

No part of this publication may be reproduced, stored in a retrieval system, or transmitted in any form or by any means, electronic, mechanical, photocopying, recording, scanning, or otherwise, except as permitted under Sections 107 or 108 of the 1976 United States Copyright Act, without either the prior written permission of the Publisher, or authorization through payment of the appropriate per-copy fee to the Copyright Clearance Center, 222 Rosewood Drive, Danvers, MA 01923, 978-750-8400, fax 978-646-8700. Requests to the Publisher for permission should be addressed to the Legal Department, Wiley Publishing, Inc., 10475 Crosspoint Blvd., Indianapolis, IN 46256, 317-572-3447, fax 317-572-4447, or e-mail permcoordinator@wiley.com

LIMIT OF LIABILITY/DISCLAIMER OF WARRANTY: THE PUBLISHER AND AUTHOR HAVE USED THEIR BEST EFFORTS IN PREPARING THIS BOOK. THE PUBLISHER AND AUTHOR MAKE NO REPRESENTATIONS OR WARRANTIES WITH RESPECT TO THE ACCURACY OR COMPLETENESS OF THE CONTENTS OF THIS BOOK AND SPECIFICALLY DISCLAIM ANY IMPLIED WARRANTIES OF MERCHANTABILITY OR FITNESS FOR A PARTICULAR PURPOSE. THERE ARE NO WARRANTIES WHICH EXTEND BEYOND THE DESCRIPTIONS CONTAINED IN THIS PARAGRAPH. NO WARRANTY MAY BE CREATED OR EXTENDED BY SALES REPRESENTATIVES OR WRITTEN SALES MATERIALS. THE ACCURACY AND COMPLETENESS OF THE INFORMATION PROVIDED HEREIN AND THE OPINIONS STATED HEREIN ARE NOT GUARANTEED OR WARRANTED TO PRODUCE ANY PARTICULAR RESULTS, AND THE ADVICE AND STRATEGIES CONTAINED HEREIN MAY NOT BE SUITABLE FOR EVERY INDIVIDUAL. NEITHER THE PUBLISHER NOR AUTHOR SHALL BE LIABLE FOR ANY LOSS OF PROFIT OR ANY OTHER COMMERCIAL DAMAGES, INCLUDING BUT NOT LIMITED TO SPECIAL, INCIDENTAL, CONSEQUENTIAL, OR OTHER DAMAGES.

Trademarks: Wiley, the Wiley Publishing logo, Cliffs, CliffsNotes, CliffsAP, CliffsComplete, CliffsTestPrep, CliffsQuickReview, CliffsNote-a-Day, and related trade dress are trademarks or registered trademarks of John Wiley & Sons, Inc. and/or its affiliates in the United States and other countries and may not be used without written permission. All other trademarks are the property of their respective owners. Wiley Publishing, Inc., is not associated with any product or vendor mentioned in this book.

For general information on our other products and services or to obtain technical support, please contact our Customer Care Department within the U.S. at 800-762-2974, outside the U.S. at 317-572-3993, or fax 317-572-4002.

Wiley also publishes its books in a variety of electronic formats. Some content that appears in print may not be available in electronic books.

Table of Contents

How to Use This Book

This CliffsNotes study guide on Jane Austen's Pride and Prejudice supplements the original literary work, giving you background information about the author, an introduction to the work, a graphical character map, critical commentaries, expanded glossaries, and a comprehensive index, all for you to use as an educational tool that will allow you to better understand Pride and Prejudice. This study guide was written with the assumption that you have read Pride and Prejudice. Reading a literary work doesn't mean that you immediately grasp the major themes and devices used by the author; this study guide will help supplement your reading to be sure you get all you can from Jane Austen's Pride and Prejudice. CliffsNotes Review tests your comprehension of the original text and reinforces learning with questions and answers, practice projects, and more. For further information on Jane Austen and Pride and Prejudice, check out the CliffsNotes Resource Center.

CliffsNotes provides the following icons to highlight essential elements of particular interest:

Reveals the underlying themes in the work.

Helps you to more easily relate to or discover the depth of a character.

Uncovers elements such as setting, atmosphere, mystery, passion, violence, irony, symbolism, tragedy, foreshadowing, and satire.

Enables you to appreciate the nuances of words and phrases.

Don't Miss Our Web Site

Discover classic literature as well as modern-day treasures by visiting the Cliffs Notes Web site at www.cliffsnotes.com. You can obtain a quick download of a CliffsNotes title, purchase a title in print form, browse our catalog, or view online samples.

LIFE AND BACKGROUND OF THE AUTHOR

The following abbreviated biography of Jane Austen is provided so that you might become more familiar with her life and the historical times that possibly influenced her writing. Read this Life and Background of the Author section and recall it when reading Austen's Pride and Prejudice, thinking of any thematic relationship between Austen's novel and her life.

Personal Background

Jane Austen's life resembles her novels—at first glance they seem to be composed of a series of quiet, unexceptional events. Such an impression is supported by the comment of her brother, Henry, who wrote after her death that her life was "not by any means a life of event." Similarly, her nephew James added in a biography published fifty years later that "Of events her life was singularly barren: few changes and no great crisis ever broke the smooth current of its course." However, just as readers find that the complexity of Austen's novel lies in its characters and style, those studying Austen herself discover that the events of her life are secondary to her compelling personality, quick wit, and highly-developed powers of observation. The fact that Austen's life lacked the drama that other authors may have experienced in no way detracted from her skill as a writer. In actuality, Austen's lack of "extraordinary" experiences, as well as of a spouse and children, probably made her writing possible by freeing her time to work on her books. Additionally, because her books were published anonymously, Austen never achieved personal recognition for her works outside of her sphere of family and friends. Such anonymity suited her, for, as literary critic Richard Blythe notes, "literature, not the literary life, was always her intention."

Formative Years

Born on December 16, 1775, Jane Austen was the seventh of eight children born to George and Cassandra Austen. The family lived in Steventon, a small Hampshire town in south-central England, where her father was a minister. The Austens were a loving, spirited family that read novels together from the local circulating library and put on home theatricals. It was for the family circle that Austen first wrote high-spirited satires—some of which later became novels after numerous and careful rewritings.

Out of her seven siblings, Austen was closest to her only sister, Cassandra. From 1783 to 1785, the two girls attended schools in Oxford and Southampton and the Abbey School at Reading. When the Austens could no longer afford the tuition, Jane and Cassandra returned home to read extensively and learn from their family how to speak French and Italian and play the piano. Most accounts agree that the Austen daughters were pretty and enjoyed the slightly limited but interesting round of country parties described in Austen's novels.

When Austen was twenty, she met Tom Lefroy, a young Irishman visiting his uncle in Hampshire. Seeing that the two young people were on the verge of an engagement, Lefroy's family sent him home rather than letting him attach himself to someone as poor as a clergyman's daughter. Austen's second brush with marriage occurred at age twenty-seven, when the wealthy Harris Bigg-Wither proposed and Austen accepted. The next morning, however, Austen changed her mind, giving up the wealth and security inherent in such a match because she did not love him. Although Austen never married, the emphasis of courtship and marriage in her novels demonstrates the impact that these experiences had on her and her interest in love and marriage.

Early Novels

From 1796-1798, Austen wrote her first three novels—*Northanger Abbey* (originally titled *Susan*), *Sense and Sensibility* (originally titled *Elinor and Marianne*), and *Pride and Prejudice* (originally titled *First Impressions*)—but none was published until later. *Northanger Abbey*, which was published posthumously in 1818, satirizes the Gothic novels that were popular at the time by presenting a heroine whose over-active imagination and love of Gothic novels lead her to see mysteries where none exist when she stays at Northanger Abbey. In *Sense and Sensibility*, published in 1811, Austen examines the contrast between two sisters who represent reason (sense) and emotion (sensibility) as they deal with being forced to live on a meager amount of money after their father dies. The threat of a father's death causing a reduced income also overshadows two sisters in *Pride and Prejudice*, which was published in 1813. In *Pride and Prejudice*, however, that threat of genteel poverty is still just a threat rather than a reality, and Austen focuses instead on how pride and first impressions can lead to prejudice.

In her early writing, Austen began to define the limits of her fictional world. From the first, there was a steady emphasis on character as she consciously restricted her subject matter to a sphere made up of a few families of relatives with their friends and acquaintances. She deliberately limited what she wrote about, and her work gains intensity and beauty from its narrow focus. In her books, there is little connection between this upper-middle class world and the strata above or below it, or consciousness of events external to it. It is, in fact, the world in which typical middle-class country people lived in early nineteenth-century Britain. The family is at the core of this setting and thus the maneuverings that lead to marriage are all-important, because matrimony supplies stability, along with social and economic continuity.

Later Works

In 1800, Austen's father decided to retire and move the family to Bath, a sea resort. Moving from the home she loved was difficult for Jane, especially because the family lived in several different places until 1809, when Mr. Austen died. During that period of nine years, Austen did not write. After her father's death, Austen and her mother and sister moved to Chawton, a country town where Austen's brother lent the family a house he owned. There Austen was able to pursue her work again, and she wrote *Mansfield Park*, *Emma*, and *Persuasion*.

Published in 1814, *Mansfield Park* tells the story of Fanny Price, a girl from a poor family who is raised by her wealthy aunt and uncle at Mansfield Park. The book focuses on morality and the struggle between conscience and societal pressures and is considered by some critics to be the "first modern novel." In *Emma*, published in 1816, Austen introduces Emma Woodhouse, the "handsome, clever, and rich" heroine who fancies herself a matchmaker. Her efforts at bringing people together, however, result in teaching her humility and her own discovery of love. Critics praise Emma Woodhouse as being Austen' most complex character, while readers find that they either love or hate Emma's story. Austen's final completed novel, *Persuasion*, was published posthumously in 1818. It deals with the broken engagement of Anne Elliott and Captain Wentworth and their second chance at love eight years later. Critics comment on the book's "autumnal feel" and note that Anne Elliott is not only Austen's oldest heroine, but also the one with the least self-confidence.

Death and Legacy

Austen lived the last eight years of her life in Chawton. Her personal life continued to be limited to family and close friends, and she prized herself on being a warm and loving aunt as much as being a successful novelist. A sudden illness, possibly Addison's disease, made her stop work on the novel *Sandition*, and she died in 1817.

After her death, during the nineteenth-century romantic period, Austen was often looked upon with begrudging admiration, as her elevation of intelligence over feeling contradicted the romantic temperament. Toward the end of the nineteenth century, however, Austen's reputation rose considerably, and she gradually gained an enthusiastic cult of admirers that were known as the "Janeites." In America, Austen was little known before 1900, but by mid-century she was receiving more critical attention there than in England. In the last decades of the twentieth century, Austen and her works received considerable attention from the general public: Most of her novels were adapted into films, modern novelists wrote sequels to *Pride and Prejudice* and endings to *Sandition*, and a mystery series was even developed with Jane Austen herself as the heroine.

INTRODUCTION TO THE NOVEL

The following Introduction section is provided solely as an educational tool and is not meant to replace the experience of your reading the novel. Read the Introduction and A Brief Synopsis to enhance your understanding of the novel and to prepare yourself for the critical thinking that should take place whenever you read any work of fiction or nonfiction. Keep the List of Characters and Character Map at hand so that as you read the original literary work, if you encounter a character about whom you're uncertain, you can refer to the List of Characters and Character Map to refresh your memory.

Introduction

Publication History and Critical Reception

Pride and Prejudice, probably the most popular of Austen's finished novels, was also, in a sense, the first to be composed. The original version, *First Impressions*, was completed by 1797, but was rejected for publication—no copy of the original has survived. The work was rewritten around 1812 and published in 1813 as *Pride and Prejudice*. The final form must have been a thorough rewriting of the original effort, for it is representative of the mature Austen. Moreover, the story clearly takes place in the early nineteenth century rather than in the late eighteenth century.

Austen's works, including *Pride and Prejudice*, were barely noticed by critics during her lifetime. *Pride and Prejudice* sold fairly well—the first edition sold out at about 1,500 copies. Critics who eventually reviewed it in the early part of the nineteenth century praised Austen's characterizations and portrayal of everyday life. After Austen's death in 1817, the book continued to be published and read with little attention from critics for the next fifty years. The few critical comments made during that time continued to focus on her skill at creating characters, as well as on her technical mastery. In 1870, probably the most significant nineteenth-century critical article on Austen was published by Richard Simpson; in the article, Simpson discussed the complexity of Austen's work, including her use of irony.

Modern Austen scholarship began in 1939 with the publication of *Jane Austen and Her Art*, by Mary Lascelle. The scope and vision of that book prompted other scholars to take a closer look at Austen's works. *Pride and Prejudice* began getting serious attention in the 1940s and has continued to be studied heavily since that time. Modern critics take a variety of approaches to the novel, including historical, economical, feminist, and linguistic.

Various critics have consistently noted that the plot development of *Pride and Prejudice* is determined by character—coincidence exerts a major influence, but turns of action are precipitated by character. Although human weakness is a prominent element, ranging from Miss Bingley's jealousy to Elizabeth's blind prejudices, outright evil is little in evidence. Austen maintains an attitude of good-humored irony toward her characters.

Historical Context

During Austen's career, Romanticism reached its zenith of acceptance and influence, but she rejected the tenets of that movement. The romantics extolled the power of feeling, whereas Austen upheld the supremacy of the rational faculty. Romanticism advocated the abandonment of restraint; Austen was a staunch exponent of the neo-classical belief in order and discipline. The romantics saw in nature a transcendental power to stimulate men to better the existing order of things, which they saw as essentially tragic in its existing state. Austen supported traditional values and the established norms, and viewed the human condition in the comic spirit. The romantics exuberantly celebrated natural beauty, but Austen's dramatic technique decreed sparse description of setting. The beauties of nature are seldom detailed in her work.

Just as Austen's works display little evidence of the Romantic movement, they also reveal no awareness of the international upheavals and consequent turmoil in England that took place during her lifetime. Keep in mind, however, that such forces were remote from the restricted world that she depicts. Tumultuous affairs, such as the Napoleonic wars, in her day did not significantly affect the daily lives of middle-class provincial families. The ranks of the military were recruited from the lower orders of the populace, leaving gentlemen to purchase a commission, the way Wickham does in the novel, and thereby become officers.

Additionally, the advancement of technology had not yet disrupted the stately eighteenth-century patterns of rural life. The effects of the industrial revolution, with its economic and social repercussions, were still most sharply felt by the underprivileged laboring classes. Unrest was widespread, but the great reforms that would launch a new era of English political life did not come until later. Consequently, newer technology that existed in England at the time of *Pride and Prejudice*'s publication does not appear in the work.

General Critique

Pride and Prejudice continues to be popular today not only because of its memorable characters and the general appeal of the story, but also because of the skill with which it is told. In *Pride and Prejudice*, Austen displays a masterful use of irony, dialogue, and realism that support the character development and heighten the experience of reading the novel.

Jane Austen's irony is devastating in its exposure of foolishness and hypocrisy. Self-delusion or the attempt to fool other people is almost always the object of her wit; note how she has Elizabeth say that she hopes she will never laugh at what is wise or good.

The reader finds various forms of exquisite irony in *Pride and Prejudice*: Sometimes the characters are unconsciously ironic, as when Mrs. Bennet seriously asserts that *she* would never accept any entailed property, though Mr. Collins is willing to; other times, Mr. Bennet and Elizabeth serve to directly express the author's ironic opinion. When Mary Bennet is the only daughter at home and doesn't have to be compared to her prettier sisters, the author observes that "it was suspected by her father that she submitted to the change without much reluctance." Mr. Bennet turns his wit on himself during the crisis with Wickham and Lydia—"let me once in my life feel how much I have been to blame. I am not afraid of being overpowered by the impression. It will pass away soon enough."

Elizabeth's irony is lighthearted when Jane asks when she began to love Mr. Darcy. "It has been coming on so gradually that I hardly know when it began. But I believe I must date it from my first seeing his beautiful grounds at Pemberley." She can be bitterly cutting, however, in her remark on Darcy's role in separating Bingley and Jane. "Mr. Darcy is uncommonly kind to Mr. Bingley, and takes a prodigious deal of care of him."

The author, independent of any character, uses irony in the narrative parts for some of her sharpest—but often unnoticed—judgments. The Meryton community is glad that Lydia is marrying such a worthless man as Wickham: "and the good-natured wishes for her well-doing, which had proceeded before from all the spiteful old ladies in Meryton, lost but little of their spirit in this change of circumstances, because with such a husband, her misery was certain."

Austen uses irony to both provoke whimsical laughter and to make veiled, bitter observations. In her hands—and few others are more capable and discriminating—irony is an extremely effective device for moral evaluation.

Dialogue also plays an important role in *Pride and Prejudice*. The novel opens with a talk between Mrs. Bennet and her husband: "'My dear Mr. Bennet,' said his lady to him one day, 'have you heard that Netherfield is let at last?'" In the conversation that follows, we learn a great deal—about Mrs. Bennet's preoccupation with marrying off her daughters, Mr. Bennet's ironic and sarcastic attitude toward his wife, and her self-pitying nature. The stage is effortlessly set for the family's introduction to the Bingley group, and the dialogue has given us information on both incidents of plot and the attitudes which drive the characters.

The pieces of dialogue are consistently the most vivid and important parts of the novel. This is natural because novels were mostly read aloud in Austen's time, so good dialogue was extremely important. We learn of the major turning points through the dialogue, and even intense inner change like Elizabeth's famous self-recognition scene ("How despicably have I acted!") is related as a person talking to herself.

Each character's speeches are individually appropriate and the most telling way of revealing what each is like. Elizabeth's talk is forthright and sparkling, her father's is sarcastic, Mr. Collins' speeches are tedious and silly, and Lydia's fountain of words is all frivolity and no substance.

The things that happen in *Pride and Prejudice* happen to nearly all readers—embarrassment at the foolishness of relatives, the unsteady feelings of falling in love, and the chagrin of suddenly realizing a big mistake. The psychological realism of the novel is revealed in the quick recognition we have of how the key characters feel.

It is very natural for Elizabeth and Darcy to be angry at each other after she first turns him down, and it is very natural for them to feel twinges of regret, and then have a complete change of mind with the passage of time. Every step in their progress toward each other is described with a sensitivity to how people feel and act. In the subtle and beautiful description of Elizabeth's self-realization is a convincing view of how an intelligent, feeling person changes.

When considering Austen's realism, however, readers should recognize that her major weakness as a writer is related to her greatest strength. She writes about what she knows—and this means that great areas of human experience are never touched on. We never see that much of the male characters, and they are rough sketches compared with her heroines. Extreme passions are usually avoided in her writing, and this becomes noticeable when, for example, she moves to a very impersonal, abstract voice when Elizabeth accepts Darcy: Elizabeth "immediately, though not very fluently, gave him to understand that her sentiments had undergone so material a change . . . as to make her receive with gratitude and pleasure his present assurances." People who dislike Austen's works often cite this lack of extreme emotions as their main reason. Even so, no one can deny her ability to create unforgettable characters, build well-structured plots, or deliver assessments of society with a razor-sharp wit. Austen's works possess a timeless quality, which makes her stories and themes as relevant today as they were two hundred years ago.

A Brief Synopsis

When Charles Bingley, a rich single man, moves to the Netherfield estate, the neighborhood residents are thrilled, especially Mrs. Bennet, who hopes to marry one of her five daughters to him. When the Bennet daughters meet him at a local ball, they are impressed by his outgoing personality and friendly disposition. They are less impressed, however, by Bingley's friend Fitzwilliam Darcy, a landowning aristocrat who is too proud to speak to any of the locals and whom Elizabeth Bennet overhears refusing to dance with her.

Bingley and the oldest Bennet daughter, Jane, soon form an attachment. Any serious relationship between the two, however, is opposed by Bingley's sisters (who do not approve of Jane as a wife for Bingley because of her mother's lower status) and by Darcy (who believes that Jane is indifferent to Bingley). Meanwhile, Darcy finds himself attracted to Elizabeth despite his objections to her family. He is drawn to her spirited wit and expressive eyes, and Caroline Bingley's jealous criticisms of Elizabeth can do nothing to lessen Darcy's admiration.

As Darcy grows more interested in Elizabeth, Elizabeth continues to despise him and is instead attracted to George Wickham, a handsome and personable militia officer. Wickham tells Elizabeth that his father worked for Darcy's father and that he and Darcy grew up together. Stating that he was favored by Darcy's father, Wickham claims that Darcy disobeyed his father's bequest of a clergyman's revenue to Wickham out of selfish resentment. Wickham's tale makes Darcy appear not only proud but cruel, and Elizabeth accepts Wickham's account without question, disliking Darcy even more because of it.

In the midst of Jane and Elizabeth's developing relationships, the Bennet family is visited by Mr. Bennet's cousin, William Collins, a clergyman who will inherit Mr. Bennet's estate when he dies because of a legal stricture known as an *entail*. Full of apologies for the entail and praises for his patroness, Lady Catherine De Bourgh, Mr. Collins informs the Mrs. Bennet that Lady Catherine has instructed him to marry and that he plans to choose a wife from the Bennet daughters. He settles on Elizabeth, but is stunned and offended when she refuses him. He quickly turns his attention to Elizabeth's friend, Charlotte Lucas, who wants to marry for security rather than love, and the two are soon engaged and married.

At the same time, Jane is dismayed to find out that Bingley and the entire Netherfield party have unexpectedly left for London. Caroline Bingley writes to Jane that they do not intend to return, and she predicts a match between Bingley and Darcy's sister, Georgiana, who is also in London. Although Jane quietly resigns herself to a life without Bingley, Elizabeth is angry for her sister and suspects that Bingley's sisters and Darcy are trying to keep him from Jane.

Elizabeth visits Charlotte at her new home in Hunsford, Kent, and meets Mr. Collins' patroness and Darcy's aunt, Lady Catherine De Bourgh, an overbearing woman who thrives on meddling in other people's lives. Soon after Elizabeth's arrival in Kent, Darcy visits his aunt with his cousin, Colonel Fitzwilliam. Darcy puzzles Elizabeth with his behavior; he seems to seek out her company, but he never says much. One day, he surprises Elizabeth by proposing to her. Still repelled by his pride and believing Darcy is responsible for Bingley's separation from Jane and for Wickham's misfortune, Elizabeth refuses him. The next day, Darcy gives her a letter explaining his role in influencing Bingley away from Jane and details the facts of Wickham's situation. A careful examination of the facts reveals that Darcy, while proud, is innocent of wrongdoing, leaving Elizabeth mortified at her discovery of how her own pride prejudiced her against Darcy.

After returning home for a month, Elizabeth goes on a trip with her aunt and uncle Gardiner to Derbyshire county, where they visit Darcy's estate of Pemberley. There they meet Darcy unexpectedly and are all surprised at how graciously he treats them. He calls on Elizabeth at her inn, introduces her to his sister, and invites her to Pemberley for dinner. Darcy is still in love with Elizabeth, and Elizabeth begins to have similar feelings for him.

In the midst of this promising situation, Elizabeth receives two letters from Jane telling her that Lydia has eloped with Wickham, causing Elizabeth and the Gardiners to leave for home immediately. Elizabeth fears that Lydia and the Bennet family are permanently disgraced and that her newly-discovered love for Darcy is hopeless. When

Lydia is found, however, she and Wickham marry. After the wedding, Elizabeth discovers that Darcy was instrumental in orchestrating the marriage, thereby saving the reputation and marriageability of the other Bennet daughters.

Bingley returns to Netherfield and soon asks Jane to marry him. Jane, of course, accepts, and Mrs. Bennet's exultation is only lessened by her irritation at Darcy's occasional presence. Meanwhile, Elizabeth's happiness for her sister is interrupted by a visit from Lady Catherine De Bourgh, who has heard a rumor that Darcy and Elizabeth are engaged, which they are not. She lectures Elizabeth on the imprudence of such a match, and then demands that Elizabeth promise not to accept any proposal from Darcy. Elizabeth refuses, causing Lady Catherine to tell Darcy about Elizabeth's impertinence and to scold him about the folly of an engagement between them. Lady Catherine's description of Elizabeth's response to her demands gives Darcy hope that Elizabeth has had a change of heart. He proposes again and Elizabeth happily accepts.

List of Characters

Elizabeth Bennet An intelligent and spirited young woman who possesses a keen wit and enjoys studying people's characters. Although she initially dislikes Darcy, circumstances cause her to reassess her negative impression of him, and she eventually falls in love with him.

Fitzwilliam Darcy A wealthy, proud man who falls in love with Elizabeth and reveals a generous, thoughtful nature beneath his somewhat stiff demeanor.

Mr. Bennet Elizabeth's ironic and often apathetic father. Unhappily married, he has failed to provide a secure financial future for his wife and daughters.

Mrs. Bennet Elizabeth's foolish and unrestrained mother who is obsessed with finding husbands for her daughters.

Jane Bennett A gentle and kind-hearted young woman who is Elizabeth's confidant and the oldest of the Bennet daughters. She falls in love with Bingley but is cautious about revealing the depth of her feelings for him.

Mary Bennett The pretentious third Bennet daughter, who prefers reading over socializing.

Catherine (Kitty) Bennett The Bennet's peevish fourth daughter, who joins her sister Lydia in flirting with soldiers.

Lydia Bennett The Bennet's immature and irresponsible youngest daughter. Mrs. Bennet's favorite, she shocks the family by running away with Wickham.

Charles Bingley A good-natured and wealthy man who falls in love with Jane. He is easily influenced by others, especially by his close friend Darcy.

Caroline Bingley Bingley's shallow and haughty sister, who befriends Jane and later snubs her. She attempts to attract Darcy's attentions and is jealous when Darcy is instead drawn to Elizabeth.

Mr. and Mrs. Hurst Bingley's snobbish sister and brother-in-law. Mrs. Hurst spends most of her time gossiping with Caroline, while Mr. Hurst does little more than play cards and sleep.

George Wickham A handsome and personable fortune hunter to whom Elizabeth is initially attracted. He eventually runs off with and is forced to marry Lydia.

Lady Catherine De Bourgh Darcy's arrogant aunt, who dominates Mr. Collins and entertains hopes that her daughter will marry Darcy.

Miss De Bourgh Lady Catherine's sickly, bland daughter.

Colonel Fitzwilliam Darcy's well-mannered and pleasant cousin, who is interested in Elizabeth, but who needs to marry someone with money.

Georgiana Darcy Darcy's shy but warmhearted sister.

Mr. Collins Mr. Bennet's ridiculous cousin, who will inherit Longbourn after Mr. Bennet's death. Upon Lady Catherine De Bourgh's recommendation, he seeks a bride, first proposing to Elizabeth and then to Charlotte Lucas.

Charlotte Lucas Elizabeth's sensible and intelligent friend, who disappoints Elizabeth by marrying Mr. Collins for money and security.

Sir William and Lady Lucas Charlotte's parents and the Bennets' neighbors.

Mr. and Mrs. Gardiner Mrs. Bennet's intelligent and cultivated brother and sister-in-law.

Mr. and Mrs. Phillips A country attorney and his vulgar wife, who is Mrs. Bennet's sister.

Character Map

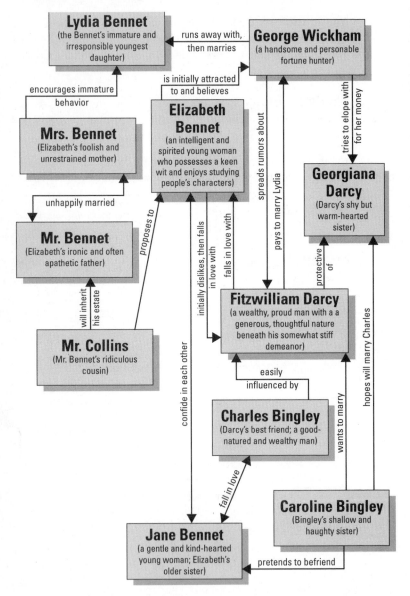

CRITICAL COMMENTARIES

The sections that follow provide great tools for supplementing your reading of Pride and Prejudice. First, in order to enhance your understanding of and enjoyment from reading, we provide quick summaries in case you have difficulty when you read the original literary work. Each summary is followed by commentary: literary devices, character analyses, themes, and so on. Keep in mind that the interpretations here are solely those of the author of this study guide and are used to jumpstart your thinking about the work. No single interpretation of a complex work like Pride and Prejudice is infallible or exhaustive, and you'll likely find that you interpret portions of the work differently from the author of this study guide. Read the original work and determine your own interpretations, referring to these Notes for supplemental meanings only.

Chapters 1–5

Summary

The residents of Hertfordshire county are excited by the news that a wealthy single gentleman named Mr. Bingley has rented Netherfield Park, a large house with extensive grounds. Mrs. Bennet urges her husband to go meet Mr. Bingley when he arrives in the neighborhood so that their five daughters may then have the opportunity to meet the gentleman and attract his interest. Skeptical of his wife's matchmaking scheme, Mr. Bennet nonetheless visits Mr. Bingley, much to the delight of Mrs. Bennet and their five daughters—Jane, Elizabeth (Lizzie), Mary, Catherine (Kitty), and Lydia.

Although Mr. Bingley returns Mr. Bennet's visit, the Bennet girls do not get the opportunity to meet him until a ball is held in the neighborhood. At the ball, Mr. Bingley is accompanied by his two sisters, his brother-in-law, and a friend, Mr. Darcy. While Mr. Bingley impresses everyone with his outgoing and likable personality, Mr. Darcy is declared to be proud, disagreeable, and cold. He especially offends Elizabeth when she overhears him refusing Bingley's suggestion that he dance with her.

After the ball, Jane and Elizabeth discuss Mr. Bingley's attentions to Jane, and Jane admits that she found him to be attractive and charming and was flattered by his admiration of her. Elizabeth comments on the difference between her temperament and Jane's, noting that Jane always looks for the good in people, a quality that sometimes blinds her to people's faults. Meanwhile, at Netherfield, Mr. Bingley, his sisters, and Mr. Darcy review the ball and the people who attended it. Although they differ in their perceptions of the ball in general, they all agree on Jane's beauty and sweet disposition.

Discussion of the ball continues when the daughters of the Bennets' neighbor, Sir William Lucas, visit. The oldest daughter, Charlotte, is Elizabeth's close friend, and commiserates with Elizabeth over Mr. Darcy's snub. Charlotte acknowledges, however, that Mr. Darcy's family and wealth give him the right to be proud. Elizabeth agrees, noting that her resentment of his proud nature stems from his wounding her own pride.

Commentary

With the first sentence of the book, Austen deftly establishes the major theme and tone of *Pride and Prejudice*. She states: "It is a truth universally acknowledged, that a single man in possession of a good fortune, must be in want of a wife." This sentence introduces the theme of marriage, which is central to the novel's plot, and also introduces the tone of irony, which Austen will use both verbally and structurally throughout *Pride and Prejudice*.

To fully appreciate the humor and artistry of Austen's novel, one must first understand what irony is and how it is used in literature. In its most basic sense, irony is the use of words to express something other than, or opposite of, the literal meaning. For example, if the first sentence of the novel is read literally, it's meaning is "Everyone knows that a single rich man is looking for a wife." However, read ironically, the sentence means something other than its literal meaning: "Everyone knows that a single rich man will be pursued by women who want to be his wife." Austen also uses irony in the structure of the plot, placing her characters in situations that seem to signify one thing and are later revealed to signify something else.

As in many of Austen's other novels, irony is employed in *Pride and Prejudice* as the lens through which society and human nature are viewed. Through the novel, Austen studies social relationships in the limited society of a country neighborhood and investigates them in detail with an often ironic and humorous eye. Note her presentation of Mr. and Mrs. Bennet, for example. Their contrasting temperaments are first shown through their manner of conversation; Mrs. Bennet chatters on while Mr. Bennet counters her talk with mildly sarcastic statements, the mocking tone of which Mrs. Bennet completely misses. After letting the reader hear the contrast between the couple through their dialogue, Austen then provides a general summary of the two parents' differing personalities. The disparity between them is amusing, but it is also ironic. In a novel about couples overcoming misunderstandings of each other to reach marital happiness, the reader's first view of marriage is one of a mismatched couple that cannot communicate.

The excitement Mrs. Bennet feels about Bingley's arrival is shared by the rest of the neighborhood, giving the reader a glimpse of the nature of provincial society. Curiosity and gossip escalate with each Bingley sighting, and when Bingley leaves to bring more new faces into

Hertfordshire, rumors about the size and composition of his group are constantly revised until he and his party make their appearance at the ball. This gossipy small town environment is a microcosm of society at large. When the narrator comments on the behaviors of the people of Hertfordshire, it can often be viewed as Austen's perspective on society as a whole.

After the ball, the discussion between Elizabeth and Jane allows their characters to become more fully developed. Jane is depicted as a young woman with a kind and generous heart who is always willing to see the best in people. More spirited than her sister, Elizabeth is a sharp observer of human nature who doesn't hesitate to make judgments. She criticizes Jane for being blind to people's flaws, an accusation which will be ironic later in the novel when Elizabeth discovers her own blindness regarding appearances and prejudices.

Austen also introduces Charlotte Lucas, Elizabeth's close friend, when the Lucas family visits the Bennets to talk about the ball. Charlotte speaks only briefly in this scene, but what she says hints at aspects of her character that will become more apparent later in the book. In discussing Darcy's proud nature, Charlotte says, "His pride does not offend *me* so much as pride often does, because there is an excuse for it. One cannot wonder that so very fine a young man, with family, fortune, every thing in his favour, should think highly of himself. If I may so express it, he has a *right* to be proud." Charlotte's assessment of Darcy's pride represents a perspective on wealth and privilege that was common in nineteenth-century Britain. As the novel progresses, Charlotte repeatedly expresses the views of society, especially in regard to money and marriage.

Glossary

(Here and in the following sections, difficult words and phrases are explained.)

a chaise and four a lightweight carriage drawn by four horses.

Michaelmas the feast of the archangel Michael, September 29.

engage to occupy or involve oneself.

It will be impossible for us to visit him In Austen's day, the women of a family could not visit an unmarried gentleman without first gaining an introduction to him through a third party, preferably a male relation.

to develop to become known or apparent; be disclosed.

mean low in quality, value, or importance.

trimming a hat decorating or embellishing a hat, as by adding ornaments, contrasting materials, and so on.

the assemblies people gathered together for entertainment.

fortnight [Chiefly British] a period of two weeks.

Boulanger a type of dance.

trade a means of earning one's living; one's occupation, work or line of business.

their brother's fortune and their own had been acquired by trade Here, the Bingleys' money has been earned by their father rather than inherited.

the liberty of the manor the privilege of hunting on the estate's surrounding land.

knighthood the rank or status of a knight.

a hack chaise a hired carriage.

Chapters 6–9

Summary

Jane and Elizabeth begin spending more time with the residents of Netherfield. Caroline Bingley and Mrs. Hurst seem fond of Jane, and the attraction between Mr. Bingley and Jane continues to grow. Meanwhile, Elizabeth finds Miss Bingley and Mrs. Hurst to be self-important but approves of their brother and the relationship that appears to be developing between him and Jane. As for Mr. Darcy, Elizabeth continues to view him as proud and reserved. She is unaware that his original assessment of her has changed and that he has begun to be unwillingly drawn to her. When he mentions Elizabeth's "fine eyes" to Miss Bingley, Miss Bingley jealously teases him about wanting to marry Elizabeth.

One morning, Jane receives a request from Caroline Bingley to come to Netherfield for dinner. Observing that it looks like rain, Mrs. Bennet sends Jane to Netherfield on horseback rather than in a carriage so that she will have to spend the night at Netherfield rather than ride home in the rain. The ploy works, and the next morning, the Bennets receive a note from Jane informing them that she is ill from getting soaked as she rode to Netherfield the previous day and will have to remain at Netherfield until she is better. Although Mrs. Bennet is satisfied at the thought of Jane spending more time in Mr. Bingley's home, Elizabeth is concerned and decides to walk the three miles to Netherfield to see for herself how her sister is faring. When Elizabeth reaches Netherfield, she finds Jane to be sicker than her letter implied, and Miss Bingley reluctantly invites her to stay with Jane.

Although Elizabeth spends most of her time at Netherfield with Jane, she eats dinner with the others and joins them in the drawing room later in the evening. While Elizabeth is in their company, Miss Bingley and Mrs. Hurst are polite to her, but when she is absent, the two women take delight in criticizing her relatives and the fact that she walked all the way to Netherfield to see Jane. Despite the ladies' disparagement of Elizabeth, Mr. Bingley and Mr. Darcy voice their approval of her.

The next day Mrs. Bennet, Kitty, and Lydia visit Netherfield to check on Jane. While they are there, Elizabeth is embarrassed by the gauche behavior of her family. Mrs. Bennet fawns over Mr. Bingley while simultaneously being blatantly rude to Mr. Darcy, while Lydia is overly forward with Mr. Bingley, reminding him that he promised to give a ball. Mr. Bingley good-naturedly agrees that he will give a ball as soon as Jane is better.

Commentary

Two features that distinguish Elizabeth from other women throughout the novel are her quick wit and her energy. In these chapters, we see her display these qualities in a variety of situations, ranging from a one-on-one chat with her close friend to a neighborhood gathering to an unplanned stay with people who consider themselves to be her social superiors. In all of these instances, Elizabeth exhibits a vigor and intelligence that appeals not only to characters within *Pride and Prejudice* but to the readers of the novel as well.

Style & Language

Elizabeth's wit is evident in her dialogue, whether she is debating with Charlotte the reasons for marriage or discussing with Darcy the existence of accomplished women. Readers get a sense of her energy from her speech, as well, as she delivers opinions and retorts with precision and speed. But Austen also shows Elizabeth's energetic nature through her actions. Throughout the novel, Elizabeth enjoys physical activity, especially walking, and readers find the first evidence of this proclivity when Elizabeth easily walks the three miles from Longbourn to Netherfield to see her sick sister. The snide responses of Caroline Bingley and Mrs. Hurst to Elizabeth's action demonstrate that such behavior is not the norm among gentlewomen.

Character Insight

Interestingly, the characteristics that set Elizabeth apart from other women in the novel are the very qualities that appeal to Darcy. He first notices that her face is "rendered uncommonly intelligent by the beautiful expression of her dark eyes." As he listens to her conversations, he is obviously intrigued by her ability to express herself and tells her that she speaks "with great energy." Darcy is also drawn to Elizabeth's "light and pleasing" figure and the "easy playfulness" of her manners. When she walks to Netherfield, Darcy feels "admiration of the brilliancy which exercise had given her complexion."

Elizabeth's appeal for Darcy becomes even more apparent in the scene in which Darcy, Miss Bingley, and Elizabeth discuss the requirements of an accomplished woman. Miss Bingley has already demonstrated her own hopes of being the future Mrs. Darcy in her comments to him and her flirtatious behavior. In this scene, however, Austen gives a direct contrast between Miss Bingley and Elizabeth as they simultaneously interact with Darcy. While Miss Bingley agrees with everything Darcy says, Elizabeth counters his statements with her opposing opinions. When Elizabeth leaves and Miss Bingley begins to criticize her remarks as attempts to attract men, Darcy reveals his own intelligent wit by subtly reproaching Miss Bingley for her hypocrisy.

Miss Bingley's behavior toward Darcy makes the reader recall the first sentence of the novel: "It is a truth universally acknowledged, that a single man in possession of a good fortune, must be in want of a wife." Austen has shown how desperately the mothers of Hertfordshire county have thrown their daughters at Bingley, and made clear that Darcy is much wealthier than Bingley. The only thing saving him from matchmaking schemes is his reserved, proud demeanor. However, his demeanor does not put off Caroline Bingley, and it is probable that he receives similar fawning treatment from a great number of aristocratic women. Consequently for Darcy, Elizabeth's forthrightness and apparent dislike of him are probably refreshing qualities in a woman. If Miss Bingley and Mrs. Hurst are examples of the women Darcy is used to dealing with, Elizabeth's spirited manner must be a welcome change, as is the fact that she is not pursuing him and his fortune.

A little knowledge of nineteenth-century society helps modern readers to understand some of Austen's ironic social commentary in this section. Miss Bingley and Mrs. Hurst take great delight in ridiculing Jane and Elizabeth's relatives who are *pseudogentry*, or professionals who do not own land, such as their Uncle Philips who is an attorney. Members of the landowning gentry, such as Darcy, or the soon-to-be-landowning gentry, such as Bingley, would consider those who earn their money through trade (a profession) to be socially inferior. Elizabeth's father is among the landed gentry, but her mother comes from a trade family. Consequently, Jane's and Elizabeth's standing in the eyes of elitists like the Bingley sisters is diminished due to their mother's family connections. However, their criticism of the Bennets is ironic, because Austen notes early on that "their brother's fortune and their own had been acquired by trade." In other words, the Bingleys' inherited fortune originates from the very circumstances that they now scorn.

Glossary

Vingt-un a card game, similar to the American card game of twenty-one.

Commerce a card game which was a predecessor of poker.

archly in an arch manner; pertly and mischievously.

complacency quiet satisfaction; contentment.

when am I to wish you joy? "I wish you joy" or "I wish you happy" was the way people in early nineteenth-century Britain congratulated someone on becoming engaged to be married.

entailed to limit the inheritance of property to a specific line or class of heirs.

milliner a person who designs, makes, trims, or sells women's hats.

tête-à-tête a private or intimate conversation between two people.

prognostic a forecast; prediction.

stile a step or set of steps used in climbing over a fence or wall.

apothecary [Old-fashioned] a pharmacist or druggist: apothecaries formerly also prescribed drugs.

draughts medicine.

retire to go away, retreat, or withdraw.

at five o'clock the two ladies retired to dress It was the custom to change into more formal clothes for dinner.

ragout a highly seasoned stew of meat and vegetables.

countenance calm control; composure.

nonsensical unintelligible, foolish, silly, or absurd.

petticoat a skirt, now especially an underskirt often trimmed at the hemline as with lace or ruffles, worn by women and girls.

not doing its office not performing its function or characteristic action.

Cheapside street and district of London; in the Middle Ages it was a marketplace.

vulgar of, characteristic of, belonging to, or common to the great mass of people in general; common.

vulgar relations Here, the Bingley sisters are making fun of Jane's relatives, who work for a living.

repaired to her room went or betook herself to her room.

loo a card game that was played for money.

playing high betting large amounts of money.

piano-forte piano.

mean ignoble; base; small-minded; petty.

solaced lessened or allayed (grief or sorrow).

temper frame of mind; disposition; mood.

prospect the view obtained from any particular point; outlook.

suffered allowed; permitted; tolerated.

mince pies pies with a filling of mincemeat.

efficacy power to produce effects or intended results; effectiveness.

tax to impose a burden on; put a strain on.

the youngest should tax Mr. Bingley Here, Lydia is placing on Mr. Bingley the obligation of giving a ball.

brought her into public at an early age introduced her formally into society at an early age. Lydia has had her "coming out" early.

Chapters 10–14

Summary

As Jane continues to recuperate at Netherfield, Elizabeth again spends the evening in the drawing room with the Bingleys, Hursts, and Mr. Darcy. She observes Miss Bingley's obvious attempts to flirt with Darcy, but Darcy seems unmoved by her efforts. Elizabeth is energized by the group's discussion of character, especially the contrast between Bingley and Darcy. Bingley, they note, is impetuous and impressionable, while Darcy is ruled by reason and reflection. Although Elizabeth frequently challenges Darcy's comments, he continues to find her more and more attractive and realizes that he "had never been so bewitched by any woman as he was by her." Only the social class of some of her relatives prevent him from pursuing the attraction.

The next evening, Jane is feeling well enough to join the group in the drawing room after dinner. Jane's attention is quickly monopolized by Bingley, leaving Elizabeth to again watch Miss Bingley disturbing Darcy with idle chatter. Eventually, Miss Bingley asks Elizabeth to walk around the room with her and then draws Darcy into a conversation with them, which soon turns into a debate between Darcy and Elizabeth over folly, weakness, and pride.

Troubled by his fascination with Elizabeth, Darcy resolves to pay her less attention while she remains at Netherfield. Meanwhile, with Jane feeling better, both Jane and Elizabeth are eager to return home. Mrs. Bennet resists sending them the carriage, so they borrow Bingley's and depart on Sunday, five days after Jane's arrival at Netherfield. Although Mrs. Bennet is displeased that they left Netherfield so quickly, Mr. Bennet is glad to have them home again.

The day after Jane and Elizabeth return home, their father announces that a visitor will be arriving that afternoon. The visitor is William Collins, Mr. Bennet's cousin and the man who will inherit Longbourn after Mr. Bennet dies. The estate is *entailed*, meaning that, according to the terms of inheritance, it must go to a male heir. Because Mr. Bennet's children are all female, the property will, by law, go to the next closest male relative: Mr. Collins. Mr. Bennet points out to his wife and daughters that Mr. Collins, as heir, "may turn you all out of this house as soon as he pleases" when Mr. Bennet is dead.

Mr. Collins proves himself to be a curious blend of pompousness and obsequiousness. He is proud of his standing as the rector of the Hunsford parish and his patronage by Lady Catherine De Bourgh, and he does not hesitate to speak at length about his (or Lady Catherine De Bourgh's) opinions. At the same time, however, he displays a relentlessly deferential manner, apologizing at length, for example, when he offends Mrs. Bennet by implying that they cannot afford to have a cook on staff. Mr. Bennet finds his cousin absurd and is amused by him, while Kitty and Lydia are shocked at Mr. Collins' announcement that he never reads novels. When he instead tries to read to them from Fordyce's Sermons, Lydia offends him by beginning to talk of something else.

Commentary

Theme

The arrival of Mr. Collins brings the issue of the entail to the forefront and helps readers to understand Mrs. Bennet's obsession with getting her daughters married. She doesn't want her daughters to get married simply for the prestige and wealth it may bring them, although that has appeal. Instead, there is a more urgent force behind Mrs. Bennet's fixation on marriage—the entail. Because Mr. Bennet has no male heirs, upon his death his estate will go to Mr. Collins rather than to any of his daughters. Because Mr. Bennet has mismanaged his money, his wife and daughters will be nearly destitute when he dies, unless the Bennet girls marry. Consequently, Mrs. Bennet hopes for a wealthy husband for at least one of her daughters so not only that daughter will be cared for, but Mrs. Bennet and any unwed sisters will be provided for, as well.

Character Insight

One of the delights of reading Austen is witnessing her remarkable skill at shaping characters into unique individuals through the most commonplace actions or events. In these chapters, for example, the development of Darcy and Mr. Collins' characters is of especial interest. The personalities of both men are revealed through similar acts—letter writing, speaking, and reading—but while their activities are the same, the manner in which they engage in the activities varies with each man, thereby illustrating the differences in their personalities.

Before the advent of devices such as the telegraph or telephone, letter writing was a very important mode of communication, as demonstrated by the large number of letters and references to letters that occur in *Pride and Prejudice*. As Darcy and Bingley discuss, one's style of writing reflects that person's way of thinking. So it is natural for someone as impetuous and changeable as Bingley to write, as his sister describes, "in the most careless way imaginable. He leaves out half his words, and blots the rest."

Darcy's writing style is quite different, though. He states that he writes "rather slowly" and that his letters "are generally long." Miss Bingley comments that he writes evenly and Bingley declares that Darcy "does not write with ease. He studies too much for words of four syllables." These characteristics of Darcy's writing style serve to reinforce and expand what readers have already gathered about him: Darcy likes to think things through and is cautious when making choices or decisions, even when choosing the right word to write. Additionally, to whom he is writing is as important as how he writes her. By writing a long, carefully worded letter to his sister, Georgiana, Darcy exhibits that he both cares for his sister and takes his responsibility for her seriously. These hints at an emotional attachment to his sister contradict Elizabeth's perception of him as cold and unfeeling. However, just as Austen's readers aren't able to read that letter, Elizabeth is not yet able to truly read Darcy.

Meanwhile, Mr. Collins also writes a letter that introduces himself not only to Mr. Bennet but to Austen's readers as well. The impression the letter gives is that the writer is a curious blend of arrogance and obsequiousness. Mr. Collins apologizes in one sentence for a breach between the families, and then brags about his patroness and his position as clergyman. He then begins apologizing again for potentially offending the Bennet daughters. Regardless of whether he is apologizing or bragging, Mr. Collins delivers his sentiments in extremely long and complex sentences. From this letter, Elizabeth can accurately assess him as a man who lacks sense.

Just as their style of writing reflects different aspects of Darcy and Mr. Collins' characters, so does the two men's style of speaking. Darcy, who is slow to write and careful of his word choice, is slow to speak and speaks judiciously, so that no word is frivolous. However, it is interesting to note how quickly this reticent man can be provoked into a fast-paced debate by Elizabeth. When Miss Bingley tries to get his attention while he is writing the letter to Georgiana, he responds with curt statements or with silence. However, as soon as Elizabeth makes a comment, Darcy begins responding at length, easily matching her intelligence and wit. His reaction to Elizabeth indicates how much he enjoys challenging and being challenged by her sharp mind.

Mr. Collins' speaking style, on the other hand, is as rambling as Darcy's is reserved. Like his letter, Mr. Collins communicates in long, convoluted sentences that range from unending apologies for some imagined slight to imperious moralizing for some perceived lapse into impropriety. Whereas Darcy usually requires someone to draw him into a conversation, Mr. Collins needs no such invitation. In fact, he generally delivers dense monologues on his or Lady Catherine De Bourgh's opinions with little concern for what others may think or want to say. It appears that the only person Mr. Collins finds more interesting to listen to than himself is Lady Catherine.

Austen rounds out the revelations of Darcy and Mr. Collins' characters in these chapters by showing the men's different approaches to reading. Darcy's extensive library at Pemberley is described earlier in the novel, indicating that Darcy and his family enjoy books and reading. Also, Miss Bingley notes that Darcy prefers the solitary activity of reading over the social activity of cards. As in the case of his writing to his sister, Miss Bingley finds it nearly impossible to distract Darcy from his book. She is finally able to gain his attention when she asks Elizabeth to join her in walking around the room. Just as Darcy is drawn out of his reticence when speaking with Elizabeth, he is also drawn out of his reading by her as he "unconsciously closed his book" to observe her moving around the room.

Mr. Collins, on the other hand, seems to have an entirely different relationship with books. His rejection of novels and consequent limiting of his exposure to books contrasts Darcy's ever-growing library. Additionally, while Darcy reads silently, Mr. Collins readily agrees to read aloud to the Bennets. Rather than selecting something that everyone will enjoy, Mr. Collins chooses a book of sermons and reads them "with very monotonous solemnity." His style of reading is just as imposing and ridiculous as his style of speaking or writing. Similarly, Darcy's style of reading reflects his reserved and aloof mannerisms.

Glossary

piquet a card game for two persons, played with 32 cards.

he . . . blots the rest Bingley writes so quickly that the ink makes blots on the paper, blurring his words.

panegyric high or hyperbolic (exaggerated) praise; laudation.

laudable worthy of being lauded; praiseworthy; commendable.

precipitance great haste; rashness.

celerity swiftness in acting or moving; speed.

aweful inspiring awe; highly impressive.

expostulation the act of reasoning with a person earnestly, objecting to that person's actions or intentions; remonstration.

approbation official approval, sanction, or commendation.

a Scotch air a Scottish song or tune.

a reel a lively Scottish dance.

felicity happiness; bliss.

gaily in a gay manner; happily; merrily; joyously.

When the ladies removed after dinner to go away. It was the custom for women and men to separate for a time after dinner. The men smoked cigars, drank, and discussed business or other subjects "unsuitable" for female ears, while the women talked and waited for the men to join them.

I shall send round my cards I will send out invitations.

propitious favorably inclined or disposed; gracious.

postscript a note or paragraph added below the signature in a letter or at the end of a book or speech as an afterthought or to give supplementary information.

laconic brief or terse in speech or expression; using few words.

flog to beat with a strap, stick, or whip, especially as punishment.

iniquitous showing iniquity; wicked; unjust.

filial of, suitable to, or due from a son or daughter.

ordination being ordained (officially installed), as to the religious ministry.

patronage support, encouragement, or sponsorship, given by a patron.

the offered olive branch peace offering.

se'night [Archaic] a week.

asperity harshness or sharpness of temper.

affability the quality of being pleasant and easy to approach or talk to.

condescension the act of condescending, or descending voluntarily to the level, regarded as lower, of the person one is dealing with; being graciously willing to do something regarded as beneath one's dignity.

discourses long and formal treatments of a subject or subjects, in speech or writing; lectures; treatises; dissertations.

quadrille a card game, popular in the eighteenth century, played by four persons.

phaeton a light, four-wheeled carriage of the nineteenth century, drawn by one or two horses, with front and back seats and, usually, a folding top for the front.

Has she been presented? Has Miss De Bourgh been brought to be introduced formally to the Queen?

a circulating library a library which loans books for use elsewhere, sometimes for a daily fee.

importune [Obsolete] to trouble; annoy.

affront an open or intentional insult; slight to one's dignity.

Chapters 15–18

Summary

Feeling a sense of obligation to the Bennet family because of the entail, Mr. Collins plans to ask one of the Bennet daughters to marry him. After Mrs. Bennet tells him that they expect Jane to be engaged soon, he decides to propose to Elizabeth. That resolved, Mr. Collins joins Elizabeth and her sisters as they walk to Meryton where Lydia and Kitty are excited to see some of the officers stationed there. Everyone's attention is drawn to a new officer—George Wickham—who impresses Elizabeth with his good looks and charming manners. As Elizabeth and her sisters are speaking with Wickham, Darcy and Bingley ride up to them. Elizabeth is intrigued to notice that Darcy and Wickham recognize each other, and as the two men barely acknowledge each other, Wickham looks pale and Darcy appears angry.

The next day, the Bennet sisters and Mr. Collins return to Meryton to dine with Mrs. Bennet's sister, Mrs. Philips. Some of the officers are also present, including Wickham, who seeks Elizabeth out and sits next to her as she plays cards. Wickham astonishes her by revealing the nature of his relationship with Darcy, telling her that his father was Darcy's father's steward and that he and Darcy grew up together. According to Wickham, he was a favorite of Darcy's father and when Darcy's father died, Wickham was supposed to have received a position as a clergyman at the rectory that the Darcy family oversees. However, Darcy gave the job to someone else—out of jealousy, Wickham presumes—and left Wickham to fend for himself. Wickham declares that both Darcy and his sister are proud and unpleasant people, and Elizabeth eagerly concurs with his opinion.

When Elizabeth shares Wickham's story with Jane, Jane insists there must be some sort of misunderstanding on both Wickham's and Darcy's parts. Elizabeth laughs at her sister's kind nature and declares that she knows Wickham to be right. As they are discussing the matter, Bingley calls to invite the family to a ball at Netherfield in a few days. Everyone is delighted, including Mr. Collins who, to Elizabeth's dismay, secures her promise that she'll dance the first two dances with him.

At the ball, Elizabeth is disappointed to discover that Wickham is absent and blames Darcy for making him uncomfortable enough to avoid coming. She is so surprised, however, when Darcy asks her to dance with him that she agrees to it without thinking. As they dance, they are at first interrupted by Sir William, who alludes to the anticipated engagement between Jane and Bingley. Darcy seems troubled by this, but is then distracted when Elizabeth raises the subject of Wickham. They discuss Wickham tensely and end their dance feeling angry and dissatisfied.

At dinner, Elizabeth is mortified by her mother's incessant chatter to Lady Lucas about Jane and Bingley getting engaged. She notices that Darcy can't help but hear her mother's loud whispers and unsuccessfully encourages her mother the change the subject. After dinner, Elizabeth's sense of humiliation grows as her parents and all of her sisters except Jane act foolishly and without restraint. Mr. Collins adds to her misery by continuing to hover near her, causing Elizabeth to be grateful when Charlotte engages him in conversation.

Commentary

With the introduction of Wickham to the novel, the plot begins to become more complicated. Note that even though Elizabeth is perceptive enough to immediately sense that something is wrong between Wickham and Darcy, her perceptive abilities where Darcy and Wickham are concerned will be blinded by her prejudice, rendering her unable to see Darcy's or Wickham's true natures.

Character Insight

Elizabeth's prejudices stem from her first impressions of the men. Whereas she was initially repulsed by Darcy's arrogant and reserved manners and his insulting refusal to dance with her, she is attracted to Wickham's "happy readiness of conversation—a readiness at the same time perfectly correct and unassuming." Additionally, Wickham further pleases Elizabeth by favoring her with his attention at her aunt's house. In other words, Wickham has behaved opposite to Darcy in his first encounters with Elizabeth, appealing to her appreciation of friendly manners and conversation as well as to her pride in being the woman he chose to sit with.

Consequently, Elizabeth's prejudice is so strong against Darcy and for Wickham that she will accept at face value everything that Wickham says. As Wickham talks about Darcy's pride, Elizabeth fails to note that her own pride is blinding her to a basic incongruity. Wickham professes to be discreet and hints that he would not defame anyone's character, but he talks extensively about Darcy. Elizabeth would not have tolerated such a conversation if anyone except the disagreeable Mr. Darcy were the subject of the talk. Austen emphasizes a theme of prejudice as Wickham imposes his prejudice upon Elizabeth and makes her even more prejudiced against Darcy, who, it is hinted, is prejudiced against all people.

Note also in these chapters the examples of the importance of manners and decorum in nineteenth-century British society. In observing the characters' behaviors and comments, it seems that in society, manners are associated with social class and accordingly with the quality of a person's character. So, for example, members of the aristocracy, such as Darcy or Lady Catherine De Bourgh, are perceived as justifiably proud in their manners because of their status in society. The Bingley sisters, who aspire to that level, are also proud and careful in their manners and distinguish with whom they associate among the Bennet family based on manners. Jane and Elizabeth, who display proper behavior, are acceptable, while Mrs. Bennet, Mary, Kitty, and Lydia, who speak and act on whim with no thought for appropriateness, are shunned. The differences in the Bennet girls' manners could be viewed from a societal perspective as reflecting the differences in their parents' class and backgrounds: Jane and Elizabeth are more closely associated with their father, a landowning gentleman, whereas Mary, Kitty, and Lydia emulate their mother, the daughter of a lawyer.

However, Austen's sense of irony comes through as she plays with this traditional societal perception of class and manners. Throughout the novel, she satirizes the manners of all classes, exposing people who have excessive pride as rude and often foolish, regardless of wealth or station. In these chapters, Austen uses Mr. Collins as an extreme example of how excessive pride can affect one's manners. In Mr. Collins' case, he prides himself on his sense of respectability, his profession, and his association with Lady Catherine. As a result, he behaves in a ridiculous fashion, going so far as to break one of society's rules and introduce himself to Darcy rather than waiting for Darcy to acknowledge their connection. Similarly, Mrs. Bennet appears absurd as she ignores decorum and talks unrestrainedly about Jane's prospective marriage to Bingley. With both Mr. Collins and Mrs. Bennet, Elizabeth acts as the voice of propriety, explaining to her unreceptive relations the proper way to behave.

The behavior of Elizabeth's family at the Netherfield ball embarrasses her because she understands the proper and improper modes of conduct at such an event. Remember also that Elizabeth's sense of etiquette has affected her perceptions of Wickham and Darcy—one man behaved appropriately upon their first meeting and the other did not. Austen's heroine seems to have a very democratic sense of proper manners, for rather than judging people by their class, she evaluates them based on how they treat others. Consequently, she likes Bingley and Wickham, who treat everyone equally, but dislikes Bingley's sisters and Darcy, who appear overly proud.

Glossary

living in England, a church benefice (an endowed church office providing a living for a vicar or rector).

the living of Hunsford the endowed office provided for the vicar or rector in the town of Hunsford.

veneration a feeling of deep respect and reverence.

obsequiousness the showing of too great a willingness to serve or obey; a fawning.

amiable having a pleasant and friendly disposition; good-natured.

represented described as having a specified character or quality.

prepossession the fact or condition of preoccupying (someone) beforehand, to the exclusion of later thoughts or feelings.

incumbent lying, resting, or pressing with its weight on something else.

folio a large size of book, about twelve by fifteen inches.

cessation a ceasing, or stopping, either forever or for some time.

muslin a strong, often sheer cotton cloth of plain weave.

commission an official certificate conferring rank.

corps a tactical subdivision of an army.

regimentals military uniform.

very pleasing address pleasing conversational manner.

game of lottery tickets a card game.

the chimney-piece [Obsolete] a decoration over a fireplace.

imitations of china paintings on china.

the fish betting chips in a game.

wonderful causing wonder; amazing.

veracity habitual truthfulness; honesty.

shoe-roses shoe laces that are ribbons tied to look like a rose.

hauteur disdainful pride; haughtiness; snobbery.

steward a person put in charge of the affairs of a large household or estate, whose duties include supervision of the kitchen and the servants and the management of household accounts.

insolent boldly disrespectful in speech or behavior; impertinent; impudent.

probity uprightness in one's dealings; integrity.

imprudent not prudent; without thought of the consequences; lacking in judgment or caution; rash; indiscreet.

her manner affected behaving in an artificial way to impress people; full of affectation.

tythes units that are one tenth of the annual produce of one's land or of one's annual income, paid as a tax or contribution to support a church or its clergy; any taxes or levies.

conciliatory tending to conciliate or reconcile (to win over; soothe the anger of; make friendly; placate).

Chapters 19–23

Summary

The morning after the Netherfield ball, Mr. Collins proposes to Elizabeth. He outlines his motivation for proposing and promises never to bring up the fact that she brings so little money to the marriage. Torn between discomfort and the desire to laugh at his officious manner, Elizabeth politely refuses him. Mr. Collins, however, thinks that Elizabeth is being coy in refusing him and lists the reasons why it is unthinkable for her to refuse him—namely his own worthiness, his association to the De Bourgh family, and Elizabeth's own potential poverty. Mrs. Bennet, who is anxious for Elizabeth to accept Mr. Collins, reacts badly to the news of her daughter's resistance and threatens never to see Elizabeth again if she doesn't marry him. When Mrs. Bennet appeals to Mr. Bennet for support, though, he states that he would never want to see Elizabeth again if she did marry Mr. Collins. Mr. Collins finally realizes that his suit is hopeless and he withdraws his offer.

In the midst of the uproar over the proposal, Charlotte Lucas visits the Bennets and learns of Elizabeth's refusal of Mr. Collins. After Mr. Collins withdraws his offer, Charlotte begins spending more time with him, and within a few days, he proposes to her. Charlotte accepts, not for love but for security, and news of their engagement outrages Mrs. Bennet and shocks Elizabeth, who cannot believe her friend would marry where no love exists.

Meanwhile, Bingley leaves for what is supposed to be a temporary visit to London, but Jane receives a letter from Caroline Bingley stating that the whole party has left for London and will not return all winter. Caroline tells Jane that they are spending a great deal of time with Georgiana Darcy and hints that she would like Miss Darcy to marry her brother. Jane is dismayed by the news, but believes that Caroline's letter is written in friendship and goodwill. Elizabeth, on the other hand, is suspicious of the role Darcy and Bingley's sisters may be playing in keeping him and Jane apart.

Commentary

Mr. Collins' proposal to Elizabeth is one of the most humorous moments in the novel. Austen has already established the absurdities in Mr. Collins' speech and manners, but his proposal raises him to new heights of pompous foolishness. Although Elizabeth at first is desperate to get away, note how she is overcome by the humor of the situation when Mr. Collins begins to speak of his feelings running away with him. There are obviously no feelings involved in his offer other than self-pride and condescension. Austen states that as he prepares for the proposal, "he set about it in a very orderly manner, with all the observances which he supposed a regular part of the business." For Mr. Collins, this is a business transaction, not the culmination of love for Elizabeth. And as Elizabeth has stated before, she wants to marry for love, not convenience.

Elizabeth's romantic view of marriage results in her feelings of shock and disappointment when Charlotte decides to marry Mr. Collins. Blind to Charlotte's practical reasons for accepting Mr. Collins, Elizabeth cannot conceive of Charlotte being happy in such a marriage.

Elizabeth's view of marriage and response to Charlotte's concept of marriage are interesting considering Elizabeth's family and future prospects. In seeking a love match, Elizabeth is searching for a relationship opposite to that of her parents. Her parents neither love nor like each other, which creates a fragmented household in which neither parent seems very happy. Perhaps Elizabeth's objections to Charlotte's realistic perception of marriage are actually objections to her own parents' relationship. However, nineteenth-century readers would understand the riskiness of Elizabeth's idealistic position. As Mr. Collins is quick to point out, Elizabeth will have a severely limited income when her father dies and the estate passes to Mr. Collins. Most young women in her situation in nineteenth-century Britain might dream of marrying for love, but would accept the necessity of marrying for security, as Charlotte does. Consequently, for Austen's readers, Elizabeth represents an ideal view of the world, while Charlotte represents reality.

Glossary

diffidence lack of confidence in oneself.

diversion distraction of attention.

purport intention; object.

dissemble to conceal the truth or one's true feelings or motives.

vivacity liveliness of spirit; animation.

one thousand pounds in the 4 per cents Elizabeth's inheritance upon her mother's death will be 1,000 pounds, which will be invested in secure government bonds that generally yield four or five percent annually.

ere before.

sanctioned authorized or permitted.

coquetry the behavior or act of a coquette; flirting.

vestibule a small entrance hall or room.

felicitations congratulations.

peevish hard to please; irritable; fretful; cross.

assiduous diligent; persevering.

abatement a lessening or reduction.

Grosvenor Street a street located in a fashionable part of London.

make their appearance at St. James St. James' Palace was where high-born young men and women were formally presented to the court, signaling their entrance into society.

coming out the formal introduction of a young woman into society.

disapprobation disapproval.

charged given instructions or commanded authoritatively.

decorum propriety and good taste in behavior.

courtier an attendant at a royal court.

rectitude conduct according to moral principles; strict honesty.

the business of love-making the wooing, or trying to get the love of, a woman.

Chapters 24–27
(Volume II, Chapters 1–4)

Summary

Jane receives another letter from Caroline Bingley and unhappily reads that the Bingleys have no plans of ever returning to Netherfield. The news leaves Jane depressed and makes Elizabeth angry. She blames Darcy and Bingley's sisters for interfering with her sister's happiness, and resents Bingley for how easily he has been manipulated by those close to him. Elizabeth's mood is lifted somewhat by frequent visits from Wickham, who continues to be attentive to Elizabeth.

Mrs. Bennet's brother and sister-in-law, Mr. and Mrs. Gardiner, come to Longbourn to spend Christmas with the Bennet family. Unlike Mrs. Bennet's other relatives, the Gardiners are well-mannered and intelligent, and Jane and Elizabeth feel especially close to them. Mrs. Gardiner cautions Elizabeth against encouraging Wickham, telling her that the lack of fortune on either side makes the hope of a match between the two of them impractical and irresponsible. Mrs. Gardiner also observes Jane's melancholy and invites her to return to London with them. Jane happily accepts and anticipates being able to see Caroline Bingley while she is there. However, after Jane is in London, a chilly reception from Miss Bingley makes her realize that Elizabeth was correct in her assessment of Bingley's sister as being a false friend to Jane.

Meanwhile, Mr. Collins and Charlotte Lucas marry and depart for Mr. Collins' parsonage in Hunsford, Kent. Before she leaves, Charlotte asks Elizabeth to visit her soon and Elizabeth reluctantly agrees. In March, Elizabeth accompanies Charlotte's father and younger sister, Maria, to visit Charlotte, whom Elizabeth has begun to miss. On their way to Hunsford, the group stops in London overnight to stay with the Gardiners. While there, Elizabeth and her aunt discuss Wickham's recent courtship of Miss King, an heiress. Mrs. Gardiner views his actions as mercenary, but Elizabeth defends his right to pursue a wealthy bride. Before Elizabeth leaves London, her aunt and uncle invite her to accompany them on a trip to northern England in the summer, and Elizabeth agrees.

Commentary

As *Pride and Prejudice* progresses, the novel's carefully balanced structure becomes more apparent. In these chapters, for example, Jane's disappointment in love is juxtaposed with Charlotte's marriage. Notice how neither situation fits with Elizabeth's idealistic view of life. Elizabeth believes that people should marry for love, not security, and has been very vocal on the subject. When faced with the reality of Jane's broken heart and Charlotte's practicality, Elizabeth responds with anger and resentment, unwilling to excuse or understand actions that deviate so greatly from her belief system. This attitude, especially toward Charlotte, is a sign of Elizabeth's immaturity and naiveté at this point in the book. As her beliefs continue to be challenged, however, she will mature.

Elizabeth's refusal to see any viewpoint other than her own is representative of the theme of blindness, or prejudice, that runs through the book. Up to this point, Charlotte has been the main person to question Elizabeth's judgment in such a well-reasoned manner that she makes the reader question Elizabeth's perceptions as well. In these chapters, though, Mrs. Gardiner enters the plot and matches Charlotte's ability to pinpoint Elizabeth's biases and inconsistencies. For example, Mrs. Gardiner warns Elizabeth against encouraging Wickham, stating "You have sense, and we all expect you to use it." She also questions Wickham's interest in Miss King, refusing to overlook the mercenary aspect of his attentions, unlike Elizabeth who readily excuses his actions. Mrs. Gardiner's concerns seem reasonable enough to make the readers wonder if Wickham is perhaps not as trustworthy and likable as Elizabeth believes him to be.

The introduction of the Gardiners to the novel presents a contrast to the rest of Mrs. Bennet's family. Unlike Mrs. Bennet and her sister, Mrs. Phillips, the Gardiners are intelligent, well-mannered, and sensitive. These differences are significant, not only because they show that Elizabeth has some relatives besides Jane that she can be proud of, but it also demonstrates that members of the middle class can be just as refined and well-bred as members of the upper class.

Glossary

repine to feel or express unhappiness or discontent; complain; fret.

solicitude the state of being solicitous; care or concern.

Encroaching trespassing or intruding, especially in a gradual or sneaking way.

circumspect careful to consider all related circumstances before acting, judging, or deciding; cautious.

impute to attribute (especially a fault or misconduct) to another.

transient passing away with time; not permanent; temporary.

crossed countered; thwarted; opposed.

jilt to reject or cast off (a previously accepted lover).

perverse persisting in error or fault; stubbornly contrary.

canvassed examined or discussed in detail; looked over carefully.

Extenuating lessening the seriousness of (an offense) by giving excuses or serving as an excuse.

candour the quality of being fair and unprejudiced; impartiality.

hackneyed made trite by overuse.

acquiescence agreement or consent without protest.

Gracechurch Street an unfashionable street.

ablution a washing of the body.

imprudence lack of prudence; lack of thought of the consequences.

duped deceived by trickery; fooled or cheated.

adieu goodbye; farewell.

mercenary motivated by a desire for money or other gain; greedy.

avarice too great a desire to have wealth; cupidity.

indelicacy the quality of being indelicate or lacking modesty.

the Lakes the Lake District in northern England.

spleen [Archaic] melancholy; low spirits.

transport to carry away with emotion; enrapture; entrance.

effusions unrestrained or emotional expression.

Chapters 28–32 (Volume II, Chapters 5–9)

Summary

The next day, Elizabeth, Sir William, and Maria leave London for Hunsford. When they arrive at the parsonage, Charlotte and Mr. Collins greet them enthusiastically and give them a tour of the house and garden. As they settle in, Maria is excited by the brief visit from Miss De Bourgh, but Elizabeth in unimpressed.

The group is invited to dine at Lady Catherine De Bourgh's residence, Rosings, soon after they arrive. Mr. Collins' dramatic descriptions of Lady Catherine and her home make Sir William and Maria nervous, but Elizabeth approaches the visit with curiosity rather than fright. As Elizabeth observes Lady Catherine, she notices that her ladyship displays tireless interests in the smallest details of life at the parsonage and in the village and never hesitates to offer her opinion or advice. Lady Catherine also turns her attention to Elizabeth and begins querying her about her family and education, and Elizabeth shocks her by initially refusing to disclose her age.

After a week passes, Sir William returns home. Elizabeth spends much of her time walking outdoors, and the group dines at Rosings twice a week. The news that Darcy and his cousin Colonel Fitzwilliam will be visiting Lady Catherine, soon generates some excitement, especially after the two gentlemen call on the parsonage the morning after their arrival. Colonel Fitzwilliam impresses Elizabeth with his gentlemanlike manner, while Darcy remains as aloof as ever.

About a week after Darcy and Fitzwilliam arrive at Rosings, the residents of the parsonage are again invited to dinner. Lady Catherine focuses much of her attention on Darcy, while Colonel Fitzwilliam seems taken with Elizabeth. The colonel asks Elizabeth to play the piano for him, and she complies. Darcy soon joins them at the piano and it is not long before Elizabeth and Darcy become engaged in a spirited conversation about Darcy's reserved behavior among strangers. Elizabeth reproaches him for not trying harder, while Darcy states that he simply isn't able to easily converse with people he doesn't know well.

The next morning, Darcy visits the parsonage and is surprised to find Elizabeth alone. Their conversation begins in a stilted and awkward manner, but soon Elizabeth cannot resist questioning him about whether Bingley plans on returning to Netherfield. Discussion turns to Charlotte's marriage to Mr. Collins, leading to a brief debate over what is an "easy distance" for a woman to be separated from her family after she marries. Charlotte comes home and Darcy soon leaves. Surprised by his presence, Charlotte wonders if Darcy is in love with Elizabeth and closely observes him in his subsequent visits.

Commentary

After Elizabeth rejected Mr. Collins and then so strongly condemned Charlotte for marrying him, both Elizabeth and the reader cannot help but be curious about how Charlotte is faring in her new role as Mr. Collins' wife. From Elizabeth's observations and the narrator's descriptions, it seems that Charlotte is settling into a marriage very similar to that of Mr. and Mrs. Bennet. Just as Mr. and Mrs. Bennet are mismatched in intellect and common sense, Charlotte and Mr. Collins also display a disparity of temperament. Where Mr. Collins is overbearing and effusive in his interactions with others, Charlotte is well-mannered and modest. When the group first dines at Rosings, for example, the narrator notes the differences between how Charlotte introduces her family and friend compared to how Mr. Collins would have handled it: "as Mrs. Collins had settled it with her husband that the office of introduction should be hers, it was performed in a proper manner, without any of those apologies and thanks which he would have thought necessary."

Additionally, like Mr. Bennet, Charlotte has found ways to distance herself from her exasperating spouse. Mr. Bennet uses his library as a retreat, and Charlotte similarly has chosen a sitting room for herself that Mr. Collins is less likely to invade regularly. Charlotte's approach to Mr. Collins is perhaps more respectful than Mr. Bennet's treatment of Mrs. Bennet, however. While Mr. Bennet responds to Mrs. Bennet's silliness with sarcasm, Charlotte does not react to Mr. Collins' inane statements. As Elizabeth observes, when Mr. Collins says something foolish, "Charlotte wisely did not hear."

Notice how differently Elizabeth views her friend's situation now. Seeing Charlotte's new home and the dynamics of her marriage has given Elizabeth a new appreciation of her friend. Whereas Elizabeth once expressed extreme disappointment in Charlotte for choosing to marry Mr. Collins, she now admires Charlotte's ability to manage her household and her husband. Elizabeth's change of heart here is subtle, but important. It demonstrates a key aspect of Elizabeth's character: the ability to change. Even when Elizabeth feels very strongly about something—in this case, Charlotte's marriage—she can be objective enough to reassess the situation and change her mind. So while she may still not agree with Charlotte's choice of husband, Elizabeth's sense of fairness allows her to eventually accept Charlotte's choice based upon her observations of Charlotte's contentment and well-managed life.

Another important aspect of these chapters is Elizabeth's interaction with Lady Catherine. While Sir William and Maria are frightened by Lady Catherine's overwhelming presence, Elizabeth is unmoved by Lady Catherine's rank or personality and instead demonstrates her ability to stand up to the woman. The establishment of this ability at this point in the book prepares readers for Elizabeth's tenacity in later confrontations with Lady Catherine.

Austen also reinforces Elizabeth's ability to verbally spar with Darcy. As seen previously at Netherfield, Darcy and Elizabeth cannot be in a room together for very long before they begin debating with each other. Although Elizabeth is entertained by Colonel Fitzwilliam, Austen shows little of her dialogue with the colonel. It is only when Darcy enters the conversation that the dialogue is written out, and then the quickness of Elizabeth's energy and intelligence are apparent in every line. In this choice of narrative versus dialogue, Austen conveys the chemistry that exists between Elizabeth and Darcy. Elizabeth may be charmed by Colonel Fitzwilliam's genial manners, but it is Darcy who challenges and stimulates her.

Glossary

paling a strip of wood used in making a fence; a pale.

ostentatious showy display, as of wealth or knowledge; pretentiousness.

sideboard a piece of dining-room furniture for holding linen, silver, and china.

fender a low screen or frame in front of a fireplace to keep the hot coals in.

vexatious characterized by or causing vexation; annoying or troublesome.

intercourse communication or dealings between or among people, or countries; interchange of products, services, ideas, or feelings.

breeding good upbringing or training.

toilette the process of grooming and dressing oneself.

enumeration the process of naming one by one, or specifying, as in a list.

glazing the work of a glazier in fitting windows with glass.

trepidation fearful uncertainty, or anxiety; apprehension.

antechamber a smaller room leading into a larger or main room.

plate dishes or utensils of silver or gold, collectively.

cassino a card game for two to four players in which the object is to use cards in the hand to take cards or combinations of cards exposed on the table.

anecdote a short, entertaining account of some happening, usually personal or biographical.

The room in which the ladies sat was backwards. The room was in the back of the house.

the commission of the peace for the county a magistrate with jurisdiction over a small district, authorized to decide minor cases, commit persons to trial in a higher court, perform marriages, and so on.

sallied forth rushed out or came out suddenly, like troops attacking besieging forces.

thither to or toward that place; there.

impolitic not politic; unwise; injudicious; inexpedient.

Chapters 33–36
(Volume II, 10–13)

Summary

Elizabeth keeps encountering Darcy during her walks through the park and is bothered when, rather than leaving her alone, he continues to join her. One day, she meets Colonel Fitzwilliam as she's walking and they begin discussing Darcy's character. When Fitzwilliam relates the story of "a most imprudent marriage" that Darcy saved Bingley from, Elizabeth infers that he is speaking of Jane and reflects upon Darcy's actions with anger and tears when she returns to her room. Feeling unfit to see Lady Catherine and especially wanting to avoid Darcy, Elizabeth decides not to go to Rosings that night for dinner, telling Charlotte that she has a headache.

After everyone has left for Rosings, Elizabeth is startled by the arrival of Darcy, who inquires about her health. After a few minutes of silence, Darcy shocks Elizabeth with a declaration of love for her and a proposal of marriage. Initially flattered by his regard, Elizabeth's feelings turn to outrage as Darcy catalogs all of the reasons why he has resisted his feelings for her—namely how her inferior social class would degrade his own standing and the problem of her family. Elizabeth in turn stuns Darcy by refusing his proposal, stating, "I had not known you a month before I felt that you were the last man in the world whom I could ever be prevailed on to marry." She condemns him for separating Jane and Bingley, for treating Wickham poorly, and for his arrogance and selfishness. He accepts these accusations without apology, even with contempt. However, he flinches when she accuses him of not behaving like a gentleman and when Elizabeth finishes her denunciation of him, Darcy angrily departs. Overwhelmed with emotion, Elizabeth cries for a half hour afterward and retreats to her room when everyone returns home.

As Elizabeth is walking the next morning, Darcy approaches her, gives her a letter, and leaves her alone to read it. In the letter, Darcy does not renew his marriage proposal, but instead addresses Elizabeth's two main objections to him: his involvement in Jane and Bingley's breakup and his treatment of Wickham. Regarding Jane and Bingley, Darcy states that he believed that Jane did not love Bingley, and he consequently persuaded Bingley that it was so, as well. He admits that he wanted to save Bingley from an imprudent marriage, but he stresses that he felt that Jane's feelings were not deeply involved because her calm nature never displayed any indication of her strong attachment. Darcy adds that Jane's mother, her three younger sisters, and even her father act improperly in public and create a spectacle of themselves.

As for Wickham, Darcy states that he is a pleasant but unprincipled man who is greedy and vengeful. Contrary to Wickham's account, Darcy asserts that he did not deprive Wickham of the clergyman position without compensation. Instead, at Wickham's request, Darcy gave him 3,000 pounds to use to study law. Wickham squandered the money, tried to get more from Darcy, and when that failed, tried to elope with Darcy's sister. Darcy directs Elizabeth to ask Colonel Fitzwilliam for confirmation of anything she questions in his letter.

At first, Elizabeth refuses to believe the letter, but after rereading it and thinking back on the circumstances Darcy recounts, she soon realizes, with a great deal of shock and chagrin, that it is completely true. Reflecting upon her former behavior and views, she is horrified and ashamed and exclaims, "I have courted prepossession and ignorance, and driven reason away, where either were concerned. Till this moment, I never knew myself." Depressed and ashamed, she finally returns to the parsonage, and learns that both Darcy and Colonel Fitzwilliam had visited and gone.

Commentary

Literary
Device

These chapters are among the most important of the novel. They present the plot's *climax*—the turning point of the action of the novel—and the beginning of the *denouement*—the resolution of the plot. Here, Elizabeth experiences her great self-revelation about her prejudices, and Darcy receives a similar blow to his own expectations and perceptions of the world.

Austen has carefully structured the plot so that Darcy's proposal comes at the height of Elizabeth's anger toward him. Elizabeth's conversation with Colonel Fitzwilliam leaves her so upset and resentful of Darcy that she makes herself sick thinking about how he has harmed her sister. Her feelings are such that she cannot bear the thought of seeing him. At the same time, Darcy's feelings for Elizabeth have reached the point of compelling him to go to her and expose his heart, leading to his outburst, "In vain have I struggled. It will not do. My feelings will not be repressed. You must allow me to tell you how ardently I admire and love you."

The proposal itself is filled with pride as Darcy refers to all the obstacles which he has had to overcome in order to make himself take this step. Rather than emphasizing his love for Elizabeth, he focuses on the negatives of the situation and makes disparaging comments about her family. Meanwhile, the proposal completely stuns Elizabeth. She has been blind to Darcy's affections for her because she has been so prejudiced against him. Note that throughout the scene, Darcy accuses Elizabeth of pride, while Elizabeth accuses him of prejudice—an ironic reversal of the way readers have viewed each character. Elizabeth tells him that he was prejudiced against Wickham, against Jane, and against things that do not fit into his social world. In turn, he tells her that she would not be so adamant "had not your pride been hurt by my honest confession." This ironic reversal emphasizes that both Elizabeth and Darcy have been guilty of both pride and prejudice.

Darcy's letter is important in three ways. First, it clarifies plot points from earlier in the book by explaining exactly what Darcy's role was in Bingley's sudden departure and Wickham's job problems. Secondly, the letter provides the reader with invaluable insights into Darcy's mind and personality. Because most of the story is told from Elizabeth's perspective, readers have little chance to know Darcy beyond his outward behavior. But the most important aspect of the letter is the impact it has on Elizabeth. Through Elizabeth's reactions to the letter, Austen masterfully displays the process of revelation and self-discovery.

Literary Device

Watch the gradual method by which Elizabeth comes to a self-revelation of her own pride and prejudice. She begins reading the letter "with a strong prejudice against everything he might say." Then as she reads the letter a second and a third time, one or two things begin to strike her as being true. After she has brought herself to accept one statement as being true, she realizes that she must ultimately accept every fact as true or reject them all. Her final realization is that she has been "blind, partial, prejudiced and absurd." Previously, she had called Jane blind, and now she has gained a moral insight into her own character and sees that she has also been blind. This, therefore, is her crucial recognition about herself. Consequently, Elizabeth's character increases in depth as she is able to analyze herself and come to these realizations.

Glossary

haunt a place often visited.

rencontre a casual meeting, as with a friend.

pales narrow, upright, pointed stakes used in fences; pickets.

tractable easily managed, taught, or controlled; docile; compliant.

prodigious wonderful; amazing.

conjecture an inference, theory, or prediction based on guesswork.

scrape a disagreeable or embarrassing situation; predicament, especially when caused by one's own conduct.

officious offering unnecessary and unwanted advice; meddlesome.

avowal open acknowledgment or declaration.

disapprobation disapproval.

tumult great emotional disturbance; agitation of mind.

plantation a large, cultivated planting of trees.

depravity a depraved condition; corruption; wickedness.

pecuniary of or involving money.

in lieu of in place of; instead of.

obtruded to offer or force (oneself or one's opinions) upon others unasked or unwanted.

connivance passive cooperation, as by consent or pretended ignorance, especially in wrongdoing.

acquit to clear (a person) of a charge, as by declaring him or her not guilty.

affinity similarity of structure.

grossest most glaring; most flagrant; very worst.

infamous causing or deserving a bad reputation; scandalous.

Chapters 37–42 (Volume II, 14–19)

Summary

Darcy and Colonel Fitzwilliam leave Hunsford the day after Darcy gives Elizabeth the letter, and Elizabeth and Maria leave about a week later. On their way back to Longbourn, they stop at the Gardiners' in London for a few days and Jane returns home with them. Back at home, Kitty and Lydia agonize over the fact that the militia is leaving for Brighton in two weeks. Elizabeth is pleased that Wickham will no longer be around.

Elizabeth relates to Jane the details of Darcy's proposal and all about the letter, with the exception of the part about Jane and Bingley. Jane responds with shock and disbelief that Wickham could have such a mercenary nature. She and Elizabeth discuss whether this new information about Wickham should be made public, but they decide against it because he will be leaving soon.

As the regiment prepares to depart, the wife of the colonel of the regiment invites Lydia to accompany them to Brighton. Worried about her sister's immaturity and flightiness, Elizabeth tries to persuade her father to forbid Lydia's going, but he refuses, implying that he would rather risk Lydia embarrassing the family than deal with her misery if he made her stay.

Lydia leaves, and Elizabeth awaits her trip with the Gardiners that summer. They leave in July and the Gardiners decide to shorten the trip to visit only Derbyshire county, where Mrs. Gardiner grew up. Derbyshire is also where Darcy's estate, Pemberley, is located. When they arrive in Derbyshire, Mrs. Gardiner decides that she wants to see Pemberley, and Elizabeth agrees after finding out that none of the family will be there.

Commentary

In these chapters, Elizabeth returns home and the story returns to some of the minor plot elements, including Lydia and the militia, Meryton's perceptions of Wickham, and Mr. Bennet's irresponsibility.

Elizabeth's most important action here is her inaction when she decides not to reveal Wickham's true nature to the public and even to keep it from her family.

However, Elizabeth does plead with her father not to allow Lydia to go to Brighton. Mr. Bennet's response exemplifies how he refuses to take responsibility for his family, especially because he knows that Lydia will probably behave inappropriately while she is there. Because Elizabeth has so recently been made aware by Darcy of the effects of her sister's indecorum, she argues strongly that the family should not allow another breach of decorum that could harm the girls' chances of finding a suitable husband. Considering that Mr. Bennet has squandered his money and will leave his daughters nearly destitute, he should be acting to help them gain the security of good marriages. However, his apathy on this matter and concern for his own comfort is stronger than any concerns he may have for his daughters. Although she cares about her father, Elizabeth is "disappointed and sorry" with his decision.

Glossary

obeisance a gesture of respect or reverence, such as a bow or curtsy.

diminution a diminishing or being diminished; lessening; decrease.

the barouche box the driver's seat in a barouche, a four-wheeled carriage with a collapsible hood and two seats opposite each other.

upbraided rebuked severely or bitterly; censured sharply.

affronted insulted openly or purposely; offended; slighted.

indecorum lack of decorum; lack of propriety or good taste.

sentinel a person set to guard a group; specifically, a sentry.

larder a place where the food supplies of a household are kept; pantry.

allayed put to rest; quieted; calmed. Said of fears or anxieties.

querulous inclined to find fault; complaining.

spars shiny, crystalline, nonmetallic mineral that chips or flakes.

acquiesce to agree or consent quietly without protest, but without enthusiasm.

chambermaid a woman whose work is taking care of bedrooms.

Chapters 43–46 (Volume III, 1–4)

Summary

Elizabeth and the Gardiners arrive at the Pemberley estate and are impressed by the beauty of the house and the grounds. As they tour the house, the housekeeper praises Darcy, saying "He is the best landlord, and the best master that ever lived." The housekeeper also confirms that Darcy isn't presently at home, but she adds that he is expected the following day. As the Gardiners and Elizabeth walk around Pemberley's grounds, however, Darcy suddenly appears. Mortified to have him find her there, Elizabeth's emotions are further confused by his courteous and gentle tone. He asks her if he can introduce his sister to her soon, and Elizabeth agrees, wondering what this show of interest and pleasant behavior can mean. As she and her relatives drive away, Elizabeth mulls over the encounter while her aunt and uncle discuss Darcy's surprising geniality.

Darcy calls on Elizabeth and the Gardiners the next day with his sister and Bingley. Elizabeth immediately notices that Miss Darcy is not proud, as Wickham had asserted, but painfully shy. Elizabeth also watches Bingley and Miss Darcy interact and is pleased to see no signs of a romantic attachment between them, as was implied by Miss Bingley. In fact, Elizabeth believes she detects several wistful references to Jane in his conversation. As Elizabeth nervously tries to please everyone with her manners and speech, the Gardiners observe both her and Darcy. From their observations, they are sure that Darcy is very much in love with Elizabeth, but they are uncertain about Elizabeth's feelings for him. Elizabeth is also uncertain, and lays awake that night trying to determine what her feelings for Darcy are.

The next day, the Gardiners and Elizabeth go to Pemberley at Darcy's and Miss Darcy's invitation. Mr. Gardiner goes fishing with the men while Mrs. Gardiner and Elizabeth join Georgiana, Miss Bingley, Mrs. Hurst, and Georgiana's companion at the house. Although Miss

Bingley treats Elizabeth coldly, Elizabeth attributes her behavior to jealousy. When Darcy returns from fishing, his behavior shows that he is clearly attracted to Elizabeth. Miss Bingley attempts to allude to Elizabeth's former attachment to Wickham and to make her look foolish by bringing up her sisters' attachment to the regiment in Meryton, but Elizabeth's calm response makes Miss Bingley look ill-natured instead. After Elizabeth and the Gardiners leave, Miss Bingley tries again to demean Elizabeth, this time by criticizing her appearance. She is deflated, however, by Darcy's remark that Elizabeth is "one of the handsomest women of my acquaintance."

Elizabeth soon receives two letters from Jane that shatter any hopes she has of further exploring her relationship with Darcy. In the letters, Jane tells her that Lydia has run away with Wickham from Brighton and that they probably have not gotten married. They were spotted headed toward London, so Mr. Bennet is going there to search for them and Jane asks that Mr. Gardiner join Mr. Bennet in London to assist in the search.

Dismayed by the news, Elizabeth rushes to get her uncle, but is met there by Darcy. Troubled by Elizabeth's agitation, Darcy sends for her uncle and stays with her to try to calm her down. Overcome by what she has learned, Elizabeth begins to cry and tells Darcy what has happened. He expresses concern and worries that his own silence regarding Wickham is, in part, responsible for the present situation. Thinking he is only in the way, Darcy leaves. Elizabeth realizes that she loves him, but fears that the family scandal will ruin her chances of his wanting her for a wife. The Gardiners soon arrive, and they and Elizabeth leave immediately for Longbourn.

Commentary

The changes in Elizabeth's feelings for Darcy that began earlier upon reading his letter continue in this section. Elizabeth began the novel disliking Darcy, and her prejudice caused her to find more and more reasons to dislike him. However, after she realized the truth about her prejudices, she opened herself up to discovering Darcy's true character. By visiting Darcy's home, Elizabeth is finally able to see Darcy for what he is. Darcy has stated that he is uncomfortable with strangers, and the only settings Elizabeth had seen him in were places that were not his home. At Pemberley, Elizabeth not only views Darcy in the environment in which he is most comfortable, but she also observes his treatment of those things and people that are under his care—his estate, his servants, and his sister. She now realizes that he is a fine brother and a landlord with a great sense of responsibility to his servants and tenants—admirable characteristics that she had previously failed to detect. Such discoveries cause Elizabeth to feel "a more gentle sensation" towards Darcy "than she had ever felt in the height of their acquaintance."

However, Darcy's dramatically altered behavior toward Elizabeth and her relatives cannot be completely attributed to his being comfortable at home. His friendly manners—especially toward the Gardiners—suggest that the confrontation between Elizabeth and himself affected him just as strongly as it did her. The magnitude of Darcy's change can be seen in his reaction to the news of Lydia's elopement. Rather than being appalled at the disgraceful conduct of Elizabeth's sister, Darcy displays tenderness over Elizabeth's feelings and well-being.

Darcy feels a sense of responsibility for the situation, as does Elizabeth. The reader begins to see here how similar these two people are in their willingness to be held accountable for their actions and their desire to protect their families. Additionally, their responses to the crisis also demonstrate how much they care for one another. For Elizabeth, although the news about Lydia is shocking and disgraceful, she shares it with Darcy, showing that she trusts him. Elizabeth also tells Darcy that she should have revealed Wickham's true nature to her family, letting him know that she believed his letter and has recognized that she was wrong when she accused him of treating Wickham badly.

Meanwhile, Darcy feels that he should have publicly dishonored Wickham when Wickham tried to elope with his sister, but his family pride prevented it. Darcy realizes that his reluctance to disgrace Wickham over his sister's near-mistake has resulted in Wickham ruining the reputation of another young woman, as well as the reputation of her family. Consequently, although Elizabeth believes that this elopement is a disgrace on her family, Darcy feels that the disgrace is on himself, a result of his earlier pride for not exposing Wickham's untrustworthiness. Even though Elizabeth has learned to love Darcy, she still obviously does not really know him, for she projects her own sense of shame onto him and believes that he will want nothing more to do with her.

Glossary

perturbation something that perturbs; disturbance.

adorned decorated; ornamented.

aspect the appearance of a thing as seen from a specific point; view.

intimation a hint; indirect suggestion.

affable gentle and kindly.

lobby a hall or large anteroom.

consigned put in the care of another; entrusted.

discrimination perception.

hanging woods a thick growth of trees on the side of a hill.

glen a narrow, secluded valley.

coppice-wood a thicket of small trees or shrubs.

acceded gave assent; gave in; agreed.

embargo any restriction or restraint.

construction an explanation or interpretation.

environs surrounding area; vicinity.

curricle a light, two-wheeled carriage drawn by two horses side by side.

livery an identifying uniform such as was formerly worn by feudal retainers or is now worn by servants or those in some particular group or trade.

acute keen or quick of mind; shrewd.

untinctured not colored or tinged with some substance or quality.

complaisance willingness to please; disposition to be obliging and agreeable; affability.

petulance impatience or irritability, especially over a petty annoyance; peevishness.

acrimony bitterness or harshness of temper, manner, or speech; asperity.

ardent warm or intense in feeling; passionate.

expedient useful for effecting a desired result; suited to the circumstances or the occasion; advantageous; convenient.

saloon any large room or hall designed for receptions or exhibitions.

brevity the quality of being concise; terseness.

post a position, job, or duty to which a person is assigned or appointed.

nettled irritated; annoyed; vexed.

direction address.

ill badly; wrongly; improperly; imperfectly.

afforded to give; furnish.

own to admit; recognize; acknowledge.

Gretna Green a border village in Scotland, where, formerly, many eloping English couples went to be married.

exigence a situation calling for immediate action or attention.

fixed firmly placed or attached; not movable.

palliation a lessening of the pain or severity of something without actually curing it; alleviation; easing.

infamy very bad reputation; notoriety; disgrace; dishonor.

actuated put into action or motion.

Chapters 47–50 (Volume III, 5–8)

Summary

As Elizabeth and the Gardiners rush back to Longbourn, they discuss Lydia's situation. Although the Gardiners are hopeful that Wickham and Lydia have married, Elizabeth doubts that is the case. She knows Wickham's mercenary nature too well to believe that he would marry someone like Lydia who has no money.

When they reach Longbourn, they find that Jane is running the household. Mr. Bennet has gone to London, Mrs. Bennet is indisposed in her room with hysterics, and Kitty and Mary are absorbed by their own thoughts. The family's distress continues to increase, especially because Mr. Bennet has not written with news of his progress in locating Lydia and Wickham in London. Mr. Gardiner leaves to join Mr. Bennet in London, and soon Mr. Bennet returns home, leaving Mr. Gardiner to manage the situation. Upon his return, Mr. Bennet admits to Elizabeth that she was right in warning him not to let Lydia go to Brighton and seems resolved to be stricter with Kitty.

Meanwhile, the whole town gossips about Wickham's disreputable nature and speculates on Lydia's future. A letter arrives from Mr. Collins condemning Lydia's behavior and advising the Bennets to disown her in order to save the rest of the family's reputation.

Relief comes at last with a letter from Mr. Gardiner informing the family that Lydia and Wickham have been found. Although they are not married, they have been convinced to do so, provided that Wickham's debts are paid and Lydia receives a small yearly stipend. Mr. Bennet agrees to the conditions, but he fears that a much greater sum must have been paid out to persuade Wickham to marry Lydia. He assumes that Mr. Gardiner must have spent a great deal of his own money, and he dislikes the idea of being indebted to his brother-in-law.

Upon hearing that Lydia is going to be married, Mrs. Bennet's mood immediately shifts from hysterical depression to hysterical giddiness. Forgetting the shameful circumstances under which the marriage will take place, she begins calculating how much Lydia will need for new wedding clothes and planning to personally spread the good news to her neighbors. When Mr. Gardiner writes that Wickham has an officer's commission in the north of England, Mrs. Bennet alone regrets that the couple will be living so far away.

Contemplating her sister's marriage, Elizabeth reflects that her wishes for a future with Darcy are completely hopeless now. Even if he would marry into a family as embarrassing as the Bennets, he would never willingly marry into a family of which Wickham is a part. This thought saddens her, for she realizes at last how perfectly matched she and Darcy would have been.

Commentary

The degree to which Mr. Bennet's apathy and ineffectualness harm his family is most clear in his response to Lydia's elopement. That he recognizes the significance of Lydia's action is obvious from his initial anger and trip to London. From what Austen has shown us of him, we know that Mr. Bennet must be extremely affected by something to be persuaded to leave his library, much less his home, for an extended period of time. However, despite his burst of activity, he is unable to resolve the situation and, turning the problem over to his brother-in-law, Mr. Bennet returns home to settle back into his former attitude of indifference. His indifference is such that, even when Mr. Gardiner writes to communicate the good news of Lydia and Wickham being discovered, Mr. Bennet goes for a walk rather than immediately sharing the news with the family. Even after Jane and Elizabeth wring the news out of him, it takes all of their coaxing and persuasion to get him to respond to Mr. Gardiner. Instead of being happy that Lydia is safe and the family's reputation is saved, Mr. Bennet frets over the financial obligation he now feels toward Mr. Gardiner.

Theme

Lydia's marriage to Wickham provides Austen with another opportunity to explore the marriage theme that runs through the novel. Remember that the last wedding to occur was Charlotte's marriage to Mr. Collins. Elizabeth disapproved of such a marriage of convenience, but her visit to Hunsford showed her that although Charlotte lacks love and respect for her husband, she is relatively happy with her home and situation. The implication there, then, is that while a marriage of convenience may not be ideal, it can be made to work.

However, Lydia and Wickham do not run off together out of love; they elope out of infatuation, lust, and necessity. Lydia believes herself to be in love with Wickham, although Austen has emphasized that these feelings did not exist before Lydia went to Brighton. Wickham, meanwhile, seems to be attempting to escape some gambling debts and capitalized on Lydia's infatuation to give himself some company. When Elizabeth contemplates Lydia and Wickham's future, she wonders "how little of permanent happiness could belong to a couple who were only brought together because their passions were stronger than their virtue"? Austen's perspective on Lydia's type of marriage, then, seems to be that a relationship based upon sexual gratification will soon lose its luster.

Theme

To understand the significance of Lydia and Wickham's rash action, it is important to realize how severely nineteenth-century British society condemned a woman who lost her virginity before marriage. Even the appearance of a loss of virtue was enough to damage a woman's reputation, thereby ruining her marriageability and shaming her family. Because Lydia and Wickham lived together for two weeks before they were found, society's assumption is that they have had sex and Lydia is therefore "ruined" unless Wickham marries her. Such a viewpoint explains why the news is such exciting gossip for Meryton and why Mr. Collins writes his letter recommending that Lydia be disowned. Although his view is harsh, it was not uncommon for families to do just that in order to save the reputations of other family members. Consequently, even though the Bennets (with the exception of Mrs. Bennet) disapproves of Lydia and Wickham's behavior, they are relieved when they are found and Wickham agrees to marry Lydia. Not only is Lydia's reputation saved, but the whole family's social-acceptability is saved as well.

Glossary

expeditiously done with or characterized by expedition, or efficiency; prompt.

profligate immoral and shameless; dissolute.

paddock a small field or enclosure near a stable, in which horses are exercised.

capers playful jumps or leaps.

frisks lively, playful movements; frolics; gambols.

sanguine cheerful and confident; optimistic; hopeful.

invectives a violent verbal attack; strong criticism.

terrific causing great fear or dismay; terrifying; dreadful; appalling.

Warehouses [Chiefly British] wholesale stores, or, especially, formerly, large retail stores.

prudence the ability to exercise sound judgment in practical matters.

faculties [Obsolete] powers to do; abilities to perform an action.

postilions persons who ride the left-hand horse of the leaders of a four-horse carriage.

post [Chiefly British] mail.

dilatory inclined to delay; slow or late in doing things.

dispirited having lowered spirits; saddened or discouraged.

procured got or brought about by some effort; obtained; secured.

licentiousness the disregarding of accepted rules and standards.

apprehending taking hold of mentally; perceiving; understanding.

augmented made greater, as in size, quantity, or strength.

heinous outrageously evil or wicked; abominable.

review an examination or inspection as of troops on parade.

copse a thicket of small trees or shrubs; coppice.

transports strong emotion, especially of delight or joy; rapture.

come upon the town become a prostitute.

secluded from the world gone into hiding because of a pregnancy out of wedlock.

situation a house, a place to live.

connubial of marriage or the state of being married; conjugal.

regulars the members of the standing army of a country.

subjoin to add (something) at the end of what has been stated.

Chapters 51–55 (Volume III, 9–13)

Summary

Soon after Lydia and Wickham marry, they arrive at Longbourn. Much to Elizabeth and Jane's embarrassment and Mr. Bennet's outrage, the couple acts completely self-assured and unashamed. In observing the couple, Elizabeth notes that Lydia seems to be more in love with Wickham than he is with her, and she surmises that Wickham fled Brighton mainly because of gambling debts, taking Lydia along because she was willing. Unimpressed by Wickham's still-charming manners, Elizabeth politely informs him that she is aware of his past but wants to have an amiable relationship with him.

One morning, Lydia mentions that Darcy was present at her wedding. Intensely curious about Darcy's involvement in her sister's marriage, Elizabeth writes to her aunt to demand more information. Mrs. Gardiner quickly replies, explaining that it was Darcy, not Mr. Gardiner, who found Lydia and Wickham, and he persuaded Wickham to marry Lydia with a substantial wedding settlement—Darcy paid all of Wickham's debts and bought him a commission in the army. Mrs. Gardiner implies that Darcy was motivated not only by a sense of responsibility but also out of love for Elizabeth. Elizabeth wants to believe her aunt's supposition, but she questions whether Darcy could still have strong feelings for her.

Mrs. Bennet laments Lydia and Wickham's departure, but the news that Bingley is returning to Netherfield Hall soon shifts her attention to Jane. While Jane claims to be unaffected by Bingley's arrival, Elizabeth is certain that her sister still has feelings for him. When Bingley visits Longbourn, Elizabeth is surprised and excited to see that Darcy has accompanied him. He is once more grave and reserved, though, which troubles her. Making Elizabeth more uncomfortable is her mother's rude treatment of Darcy, especially when she reflects upon how much Darcy has secretly helped the Bennet family.

Darcy goes to London and Bingley continues to visit the Bennets. He and Jane grow closer, and much to everyone's delight, he finally proposes.

Commentary

Character Insight

Darcy completely wins Elizabeth over with his involvement in Lydia's marriage. She is ashamed to think of how much he has done for her family, but she is also deeply grateful for his assistance and is intrigued by his possible motivations. Note that despite the fact that Elizabeth has recognized how well-suited she and Darcy are and that she recognizes his generous and thoughtful nature, she still does not believe he can overcome the detriments of her family, especially now that Wickham is her brother-in-law. At this point, Darcy has proven his willingness to sacrifice a little pride for Elizabeth's happiness, especially in his dealings with Wickham. So perhaps Elizabeth's inability to believe in the magnitude of his love for her stems not from any fault of Darcy's, but rather from Elizabeth's own insecurities regarding her family and her seemingly pointless hopes for a life with Darcy. These insecurities paired with the intensity of her feelings for Darcy cause her to do something extremely uncharacteristic—she does not confide in Jane. Considering that she shares everything with Jane except potentially painful matters concerning Bingley, Elizabeth's silence on such important, life-altering matters is significant and seems to indicate the depth of her uncertainty.

Elizabeth's insecurities are not relieved at all by Darcy's visit to Longbourn with Bingley. His retreat into silence frustrates and confuses her, but instead of attributing his reticence to pride, Elizabeth fairly considers that "perhaps he could not in her mother's presence be what he was before her uncle and aunt."

Literary Device

Austen cleverly builds the reader's sense of anticipation to mirror Elizabeth's as she is continuously prevented from speaking with Darcy. Throughout the novel, Austen has conditioned the reader to expect witty, intelligent, and rapid dialogue between Elizabeth and Darcy in the scenes in which they are together. She has made their exchanges central to the development of the characters and the plot. When Austen restricts their ability to interact here, she withholds one of the most enjoyable aspects of their relationship. The result of this technique is a heightened identification with Elizabeth and Darcy's obvious frustration as they are forced to prolong their uncertainty and suspense regarding their feelings for each other.

Unable to question Darcy about his attitude toward Bingley and Jane, Elizabeth instead watches closely as Bingley's presence revitalizes the relationship between him and her sister. Earlier, Darcy had objected to Jane and Bingley's marriage, but now as he accompanies his friend to the Bennets' home, it seems as if he is encouraging it. Elizabeth is not certain, but she feels strongly that Darcy is using his influence to bring about a proposal. Darcy's apparent support of Jane and Bingley's relationship again emphasizes the reversal that Darcy has undergone.

Austen's marriage theme, which up to this point has been a bit bleak, becomes more positive with Jane and Bingley's engagement. Finally, readers witness a love match, one of the few happy marriages in the novel. Jane and Bingley's relationship is based on genuine love, understanding, and a similarity of feelings and perspectives on the world. Such a relationship stands in obvious contrast to the marriages of the Bennets, the Collinses, and the Wickhams, which all lack this type of emotion or compatibility. From the beginning of the novel, both Jane and Elizabeth have repeatedly stated that they want to marry for love. From the indisputable happiness caused by Jane's engagement, it seems that Jane and Elizabeth's view of marriage is the one approved of by Austen. Such a marriage naturally enhances the lives of the couple, but it also enriches the lives of their family, friends, and future children.

Glossary

alacrity eager willingness or readiness.

austerity a severe or stern look or manner; forbidding quality.

parade to walk about ostentatiously; show off.

the first of September the beginning of bird-hunting season.

distracted insane; crazy.

cogent forceful and to the point, as a reason or argument; convincing.

stratagems tricks or schemes for achieving some purpose.

comprise to include; contain.

racked to trouble, torment, or afflict.

imputed to attribute (especially a fault or misconduct) to another.

quit to leave; depart from.

obstinate unreasonably determined to have one's own way; stubborn.

attendant accompanying as a circumstance or result.

supplication a humble request, prayer, or petition.

abominate to feel hatred and disgust for; loathe.

liberality willingness to give or share freely; generosity.

saucy rude; impudent.

gallantry the courtly manner of one who is stylish.

twelvemonth [Chiefly British, archaic] one year.

simpers smiles in a silly, affected, or self-conscious way.

prodigiously in a way indicating great size, power, or extent; enormously; hugely.

canvassed examined or discussed in detail; looked over carefully.

tidings news; information.

partake to take part (in an activity); participate.

covies small flocks or broods of birds.

hither to or toward this place; here.

sanction support; encouragement; approval.

confederacy people united for some common purpose.

abhorrent causing disgust or hatred; detestable.

rapacity greed; voraciousness.

concurrence agreement; accord.

solicitude the state of being solicitous; care or concern.

circumspection cautiousness; carefulness.

cordiality cordial quality; warm, friendly feeling.

panegyric a formal speech or piece of writing praising a person or event.

Chapters 56–60 (Volume III, 14–19)

Summary

Lady Catherine De Bourgh unexpectedly drops by Longbourn one day to talk to Elizabeth. She has heard a rumor that Darcy and Elizabeth are or are about to be engaged and is determined to stop any romance that may exist between them. Declaring that Darcy and Miss De Bourgh have been intended for each other since they were born, Lady Catherine tells Elizabeth that the match between her nephew and daughter will not be ruined by "a young woman of inferior birth, of no importance in the world, and wholly unallied to the family." Despite Lady Catherine's demands, Elizabeth refuses to be intimidated and she fuels Lady Catherine's outrage by refusing to promise never to accept a proposal from Darcy. Lady Catherine leaves angrily, threatening to approach Darcy on the matter. Shaken by the confrontation, Elizabeth wonders how Darcy will react to his aunt's denunciation of her. She decides that if Darcy does not return to Netherfield, she will know that he has submitted to his aunt's wishes.

The next morning, Mr. Bennet asks Elizabeth into his library, where he shares a letter with her that he received from Mr. Collins. In it, Mr. Collins also addresses the rumored engagement between Elizabeth and Darcy and warns his cousin against it, stating that Lady Catherine does not approve. Mr. Bennet finds the idea of Elizabeth being engaged to Darcy ludicrous and tries to get Elizabeth to laugh with him over the situation, while Elizabeth miserably listens and tries to think of something to say.

Several days later, contrary to Elizabeth's expectations, Darcy comes to Longbourn with Bingley. She and Darcy go for a walk and Elizabeth blurts out her thanks for his involvement in Lydia and Wickham's marriage. In turn, Darcy declares that he still loves Elizabeth and wants to marry her. When Elizabeth responds that her feelings have greatly changed and that she also loves him, Darcy is delighted and the two happily discuss the history of their relationship. Darcy tells Elizabeth that her refusal of his first proposal caused him to examine his pride and prejudices and to subsequently alter his behavior. They also discuss Bingley and Jane. Darcy is happy about their engagement, and he admits to encouraging Bingley to propose.

Darcy and Elizabeth's engagement is so unexpected that the Bennet family has difficulty believing it at first. Elizabeth's criticisms of Darcy were initially so strong that no one except the Gardiners had any idea of the change in her feelings for him. After the family is convinced, however, everyone's reactions are characteristic. Jane is genuinely happy for her sister, and Mrs. Bennet is thrilled at the prospect of Darcy's wealth. Mr. Bennet is saddened that his favorite daughter will be leaving, but he is happy to discover that Darcy paid off Wickham rather than Mr. Gardiner, feeling that, because a family member did not pay the debt, Mr. Bennet is released from his obligation to pay the money back.

After the marriages of Elizabeth and Darcy and Jane and Bingley, life progresses happily for the newlyweds. The Bingleys move close to Pemberley after about a year, and Elizabeth and Jane are frequently visited by their sister Kitty, who improves considerably under their influence. Back at Longbourn, Mrs. Bennet continues to be silly, Mr. Bennet misses Elizabeth and enjoys visiting her, and Mary appreciates having no pretty sisters at home to compete with. As for the rest of their families, Wickham and Lydia continue to squander money, Lady Catherine is cold to Elizabeth, and Miss Darcy and Elizabeth become very close. Darcy and Elizabeth's happiness is increased by visits from the Gardiners, whom Darcy and Elizabeth feel are responsible for bringing them together.

Commentary

The confrontation between Elizabeth and Lady Catherine underscores Elizabeth's ability to hold her own with those aristocrats whose pride will make them prejudiced against her when she becomes Darcy's wife. From the beginning of the novel, Elizabeth was shown to be capable of resisting others' wills and clearly articulating her beliefs. However, Elizabeth's maturation process has given her a deeper understanding of herself and of others, and as a result she is able to deal with adversity in a much calmer, less confrontational manner. Since she had her self-revelation, Elizabeth has controlled potentially volatile situations with complete confidence. She deflated Miss Bingley's attempts to provoke her at Pemberley, put Wickham in his place after he married Lydia, and now easily routs her most challenging adversary, Lady Catherine De Bourgh.

The ironic result of Lady Catherine's visit is to insure the marriage between Darcy and Elizabeth. Lady Catherine came in order to prevent it, but when Darcy hears the manner in which Elizabeth answered her, he realizes that Elizabeth's feelings must have changed in some degree. If she had felt as she did when she told him that he was "the last man in the world whom I could ever be prevailed on to marry," she certainly would not have refused to say she would never accept a proposal from him. Although Elizabeth and Darcy probably would have eventually made their feelings known to each other without Lady Catherine's meddling, her interference helps to expedite the process.

Austen resolves the plot tidily, wrapping up all of the storylines with a brief snapshot of the characters' futures. Most important of those futures, of course, are the successful marriages of Elizabeth and Jane. Austen's structural symmetry is evident in her concluding the novel with Elizabeth and Darcy's engagement and vision of their life together. In the beginning of the book, Austen presents the reader with the image of the Bennets' unhappy marriage and the sense of a perilous future for the Bennet daughters if they remain unwed. The difficulty of the situation for the young women was that they did not want unhappy marriages, which they knew first-hand to be a miserable way to spend one's life, but they also knew that if they did not marry, eventually they would be homeless and poor and would live miserably on the charity of other family members. As a result, the driving force behind the plot is for the Bennet girls—Jane and Elizabeth in particular—to find husbands they can love and respect.

Jane finds her ideal mate almost immediately, but circumstances keep them apart until almost the end of the novel. Elizabeth also immediately finds the man who will be her husband, but they both need to undergo a process of self-discovery before they can truly understand each other and have a successful marriage. Out of all the engagements and marriages that occur in the book, Elizabeth's takes the longest to come about. In the end, it also seems that her marriage will be the richest emotionally, intellectually, and monetarily—the exact opposite of her parents' marriage. Consequently, Austen concludes her novel with an implied message that marital happiness originates not from a love of security

(Charlotte), passion (Lydia), or perfect harmony (Jane), but rather from an honest recognition and love of the whole person, strengths and weaknesses. Before people can find that kind of complete understanding of another, however, they must first fully know themselves.

Glossary

equipage a carriage, especially one with horses and liveried servants.

the horses were post The horses were normally used by postal carriers but could also be rented out to people who did not want to use their own horses for a journey.

hermitage a secluded retreat.

parasol a lightweight umbrella carried by women as a sunshade.

industriously with earnest, steady effort; in a diligent manner.

foundation the fundamental principle on which something is founded; basis.

borne put up with; tolerated.

he was destined for his cousin The marriage of cousins was an acceptable way to keep wealth and estates within aristocratic families.

tacit not expressed or declared openly, but implied or understood.

brooking putting up with; enduring: usually in the negative.

sphere social stratum, place in society, or walk of life.

incensed made very angry.

oblige to do a favor or service.

prodigiously wonderfully or amazingly.

incessantly never ceasing; continuing or being repeated without stopping or in a way that seems endless.

meditate to plan or intend.

enumerating naming one-by-one; specifying, as in a list.

penetration the act or power of discerning.

sagacity the quality or an instance of being sagacious; penetrating intelligence and sound judgment.

incur to become subject to through one's own action; bring upon oneself.

vice evil or wicked conduct or behavior; depravity or corruption.

denoted was a sign of; indicated.

irrevocably in a way that cannot be revoked, recalled, or undone; unalterably.

frankness the quality of being open and honest in expressing what one thinks or feels; straightforwardness.

abhorrence an abhorring; loathing; detestation.

annexed joined; connected.

devoid completely without; empty or destitute (of).

reproofs things said in reproving; rebukes.

gravity solemnity or sedateness of manner or character; earnestness.

narrowly close; careful; minute; thorough.

epithet an adjective, noun, or phrase, often specif. a disparaging one, used to characterize some person or thing.

vehemence intense feeling or strong passion; fervent or impassioned state or condition.

pin-money [Archaic] an allowance of money given to a wife for small personal expenses.

special license a prestigious type of marriage license that was obtained from a bishop or archbishop.

heedless not taking heed; careless; unmindful.

Discharging getting rid of; acquitting oneself of; paying (a debt) or performing (a duty).

arrear an unpaid and overdue debt; usually in the plural.

CHARACTER ANALYSES

The following critical analyses delve into the physical, emotional, and psychological traits of the literary work's major characters so that you might better understand what motivates these characters. The writer of this study guide provides this scholarship as an educational tool by which you may compare your own interpretations of the characters. Before reading the character analyses that follow, consider first writing your own short essays on the characters as an exercise by which you can test your understanding of the original literary work. Then, compare your essays to those that follow, noting discrepancies between the two. If your essays appear lacking, that might indicate that you need to re-read the original literary work or re-familiarize yourself with the major characters.

Elizabeth Bennet

Even in her blindest moments, Elizabeth Bennet is an unfailing attractive character. She is described as a beauty and has especially expressive eyes, but what everybody notices about her is her spirited wit and her good sense. Mainly because of that good sense, Elizabeth is her father's favorite child and her mother's least favorite. Her self-assurance comes from a keen critical mind and is expressed through her quick-witted dialogue.

Elizabeth's sparkling and teasing wit brings on Lady Catherine's disapproval and Darcy's admiration. She is always interesting to listen to and always ready to laugh at foolishness, stating, "I hope I never ridicule what is wise or good. Follies and nonsense, whims and inconsistencies *do* divert me, I own, and I laugh at them whenever I can." Because of her exceptional powers of observation, Elizabeth's sense of the difference between the wise and foolish, for the most part, is very good.

In spite of her mistake in misjudging Wickham and Darcy, and her more blamable fault of sticking stubbornly to that judgment until forced to see her error, Elizabeth is usually right about people. For example, she painfully recognizes the inappropriate behavior of most of her family, and she quickly identifies Mr. Collins as a fool and Lady Catherine as a tyrant. However, this ability to size people up leads her too far at times. She proceeds from reasonable first impressions of Darcy and Wickham to definite and wrong conclusions about their characters. Her confidence in her own discernment—a combination of both pride and prejudice—is what leads her into her worst errors.

Fitzwilliam Darcy

Darcy exhibits all the good and bad qualities of the ideal English aristocrat—snobbish and arrogant, he is also completely honest and sure of himself. Darcy is not actually a titled nobleman, but he is one of the wealthiest members of the landed gentry—the same legal class that Elizabeth's much poorer family belongs to. While Darcy's sense of social superiority offends people, it also promotes some of his better traits. As Wickham notes in his sly assessment, "His pride never deserts him; but with the rich, he is liberal-minded, just, sincere, rational, honorable, and perhaps agreeable—allowing for fortune and figure."

It is, in fact, his ideal of nobility that makes Darcy truly change in the novel. When Elizabeth flatly turns down his marriage proposal and tells him that it was ungentlemanly, Darcy is startled into realizing just how arrogant and assuming he has been. He reflects later on why he was that way: "I was spoiled by my parents, who though good themselves . . . allowed, encouraged, almost taught me to be selfish and overbearing . . . to think meanly of all the rest of the world." Darcy's humbling makes him more sensitive to what other people feel. In the end, he is willing to marry into a family with three silly daughters, an embarrassing mother, and Wickham as a brother-in-law. It may be that he becomes more easygoing about other people's faults because he is now aware of his own.

Jane Bennet

The oldest and most beautiful of the Bennet daughters, Jane has a good heart and a gentle nature. As Elizabeth's confidant, Jane helps to keep her sister's tendency to be judgmental in check by offering positive interpretations of negative situations. Jane's desire to see only the best in people becomes rather extreme at times, as in her disbelief that Wickham could be a liar, but she is not so entrenched in her world view that her opinion cannot be changed. Take, for example, her relationship with Caroline Bingley. When Jane finally recognizes Miss Bingley's insincerity, she stops making excuses for her and does not pursue the friendship. However, when she and Miss Bingley become sisters-in-law, Jane's good nature causes her to receive Miss Bingley's friendly overtures with more responsiveness than Miss Bingley deserves.

Although Jane enters into one of the happiest and most successful marriages in the novel, her relationship with Bingley is a rather static one. Just as she is consistently good and kind, her feelings and regard for Bingley never falter or change. She feels sorrow when he leaves, of course, but that does not diminish her love for him. Their relationship, while pleasant, is not marked by the range of emotions that Elizabeth and Darcy feel for one another. Her marriage, then, is favorable because she and Bingley married for love and are compatible, but it is not quite ideal because it lacks the depth found in Elizabeth and Darcy's marriage.

Mr. Bennet

Mr. Bennet is one of the least mobile characters in the book. In a novel in which people are active visiting neighbors or going on trips, Mr. Bennet is rarely seen outside of his library. His physical retreat from the world signifies his emotional retreat from his family. Although he is an intelligent man, he is lazy and apathetic and chooses to spend his time ridiculing the weaknesses of others rather than addressing his own problems. His irresponsibility has placed his family in the potentially devastating position of being homeless and destitute when he dies. He recognizes this fact, but does nothing to remedy the situation, transforming him from a character who is simply amusing into someone whom readers cannot help but feel some degree of contempt for.

Mrs. Bennet

Silly, emotional, and irrational, Mrs. Bennet's behavior does more to harm her daughters' chances at finding husbands than it does to help. She encourages Kitty and Lydia's bad behavior and her attempts to push Elizabeth into an unwanted marriage with Mr. Collins show her to be insensible of her children's aversion to a loveless marriage. Mrs. Bennet is concerned with security rather than happiness, as demonstrated by her own marriage to a man she cannot understand and who treats her with no respect.

Lydia Bennet

Emotional and immature, Lydia is the Bennet daughter who most takes after her mother. Lydia's misbehavior stems from a lack of parental supervision on the parts of both her mother and father. Her marriage to Wickham represents a relationship that is based on physical gratification. Lydia does not think, she simply acts upon her impulses, and that impulsiveness, combined with negligent parents, leads to her near ruin.

George Wickham

A charming and well-spoken young man, Wickham uses his charisma to insinuate himself into the lives of others. His behavior throughout the novel shows him to be a gambler who has no scruples about running up his debts and then running away. His mercenary nature regarding women is first noted by Mrs. Gardiner, who comments on his sudden interest in Miss King. Like Elizabeth, he possesses an ability to read people; however, he uses this knowledge to his advantage. When he finds that Elizabeth dislikes Darcy, for example, he capitalizes on her dislike to gain her sympathies.

Charlotte Lucas (later Collins)

Although Charlotte's marriage of convenience to Mr. Collins is criticized by Elizabeth, her situation and marriage is much more realistic than is Elizabeth's for nineteenth-century Britain. Elizabeth's story is a work of romantic fiction, but Charlotte's is a mirror of reality. Even though Elizabeth cannot understand Charlotte's reasons for marrying Mr. Collins, she does respect Charlotte's sound management of her household and her ability to see as little of Mr. Collins as possible. Whereas Elizabeth's relationship with Darcy was what Austen's female readers may dream of, Charlotte's marriage to Mr. Collins was the actual life they would most likely have to face.

CRITICAL ESSAYS

On the pages that follow, the writer of this study guide provides critical scholarship on various aspects of Austen's Pride and Prejudice. These interpretive essays are intended solely to enhance your understanding of the original literary work; they are supplemental materials and are not to replace your reading of Pride and Prejudice. When you're finished reading Pride and Prejudice, and prior to your reading this study guide's critical essays, consider making a bulleted list of what you think are the most important themes and symbols. Write a short paragraph under each bullet explaining why you think that theme or symbol is important; include at least one short quote from the original literary work that supports your contention. Then, test your list and reasons against those found in the following essays. Do you include themes and symbols that the study guide author doesn't? If so, this self test might indicate that you are well on your way to understanding original literary work. But if not, perhaps you will need to re-read Pride and Prejudice.

Women's Roles in Early Nineteenth-Century Britain

The importance of marriage in the lives of Elizabeth Bennet and her sisters may be difficult for modern readers to understand. Young women today have a variety of options open to them regarding their future—they can marry, of course, but they can also go to college, follow any career path that may interest them, and live on their own, independent of relatives or chaperones. Young women of Austen's day did not have these advantages. Although the daughters of the middle and upper class could be sent to school, their education there consisted more of becoming "accomplished" than it did of expanding their academic knowledge. Additionally, women in early nineteenth-century Britain were not allowed in higher education, so private tutors, governesses, and private schools were the extent of structured education open to them. Naturally, a young woman like Elizabeth Bennet with a lively, inquisitive mind would have been able to further her education independently through reading. Elizabeth indicates as much to Lady Catherine, describing education for her and her sisters as being unstructured but accessible: "such of us as wished to learn, never wanted the means. We were always encouraged to read, and had all the masters that were necessary. Those who chose to be idle certainly might." In discussing a woman's accomplishments, Darcy also comments that a really commendable woman will improve "her mind by extensive reading."

A woman's formal education was limited because her job opportunities were limited—and vice versa. Society could not conceive of a woman entering a profession such as medicine or the law and therefore did not offer her the chance to do so. In fact, middle- and upper-class women had few avenues open to them for a secure future. If unmarried, they would remain dependent upon their relatives, living with or receiving a small income from their fathers, brothers, or other relations who could afford to support them. In Elizabeth's case, she is dependent upon her father while he is living and she is unmarried, but because of the entail and the fact that she has no brothers, her situation could become quite desperate when he dies. She and her mother and sisters would be forced to rely upon the charity of their relatives, such as Mr. and Mrs. Phillips, Mr. and Mrs. Gardiner, and even Mr. Collins. Such a position would be extremely distasteful and humiliating.

Other options available to a gently bred young woman who needs to support herself would be to take a position as a governess or a lady's companion. Both jobs allowed a woman to earn a living without sacrificing her social position. However, the working conditions of these jobs were often unpleasant and degrading. Governesses might be preyed upon by the men in the family for which they worked, while lady's companions, such as Miss De Bourgh's companion, Mrs. Jenkinson, might be treated poorly by their employers and given menial tasks to attend to. Any other form of employment a woman could take was considered unacceptable and would most likely irrevocably harm her social standing.

An unmarried woman's social standing would also be harmed by her living alone, outside of the sphere of her family's influence. If a single woman who had never been married was not living with her family, she should at least be living with a suitable chaperone. Therefore, when the Bennet daughters travel in *Pride and Prejudice*, they always stay in the company of a relative or a respectable married woman. Jane visits the Gardiners, Elizabeth stays with the now-married Charlotte, Elizabeth later travels with the Gardiners, and Lydia goes to Brighton as the guest of Mrs. Forster. When Lydia runs away with Wickham, however, her reputation and social standing are ruined by the fact that she lived with him alone and unwed for two weeks. Only marriage can save her from being rejected by her social sphere, and only marriage can save her family's reputation as well, unless they disowned her. Consequently, Darcy's efforts to find Wickham and Lydia and to buy Wickham's marriage to Lydia quite literally saves not only Lydia's reputation, but the whole Bennet family as well.

Money in *Pride and Prejudice*

Money plays a central role to the plot of *Pride and Prejudice*. Because of the entail, the Bennet women will have a bleak financial future after Mr. Bennet dies. When readers recognize this, Mrs. Bennet's pursuit of husbands for her daughters takes on a sense of urgency that supercedes her foolish behavior. Translating the monetary realities that the characters of *Pride and Prejudice* face into modern equivalents helps readers to better understand the characters' motivations and the significance of their actions.

Austen describes people's financial situations throughout *Pride and Prejudice* in terms of actual monetary amounts. Darcy is not simply rich, he has 10,000 pounds a year. When Elizabeth's father dies, she will not only be poor, she will have a mere 40 pounds a year. But what do these figures mean in modern U.S. dollars? Critic Edward Copeland has calculated the value of one pound in Austen's day to be roughly equivalent to 80 dollars now. While he emphasizes that his estimate is not scientific and is probably conservative, such an equivalency helps to put the sums Austen scatters throughout the novel into perspective.

According to Austen, Mr. Bennet's annual income is 2,000 pounds, or 160,000 dollars. Compare that to Darcy's 10,000 pounds or 800,000 dollars. Additionally, the sums Austen gives are often discussed in terms of 4 or 5 percents. These percents refer to the fact that the income the landed gentry earned came from investing their money in secure government bonds. Therefore, Bingley is described as having "four or five thousand a year" because Mrs. Bennet is not sure of what his 100,000 pound inheritance is earning. Similarly, Mr. Collins assumes the lesser amount when he condescendingly informs Elizabeth that he will not reproach her for bringing only "one thousand pounds in the 4 per cents" to their marriage. In other words, Elizabeth will only have a 40 or 50 pound annual income to live off of after her father dies, which translates into 3,200 or 4,000 dollars.

This comparison of Austen's pound with the modern dollar not only clarifies characters' annual incomes, but also exposes the magnitude of certain financial transactions, such as Darcy's dealings with Wickham. First, Wickham inherited 1,000 pounds, or 80,000 dollars from Darcy's father. After dissolving his claim to the clergyman position, Wickham received 3,000 more pounds (240,000 dollars) from Darcy. Within three years, he was again asking Darcy for money, which Darcy refused to give him. Wickham then attempts to elope with Miss Darcy, whose inheritance totals 30,000 pounds (2.4 million dollars). Wickham then runs off with Lydia, whose portion equals Elizabeth's—40 pounds a year, 1,000 pounds overall. He tells Darcy that he has no intention of marrying Lydia and still plans to marry an heiress. To persuade Wickham to marry Lydia, Darcy must then pay Wickham's debts, totaling 1,000 pounds, or 80,000 dollars in addition to buying his commission at about 450 pounds or 36,000 dollars. Mr. Bennet also conjectures that "Wickham's a fool if he takes her for less than ten thousand pounds," meaning that Darcy probably also paid Wickham an additional 800,000 dollars. Elizabeth's overwhelming gratitude toward Darcy and the debt of her family to him become much clearer in light of these figures in U.S. dollars.

CliffsNotes Review

Use this CliffsNotes Review to test your understanding of the original text, and reinforce what you've learned in this book. After you work through the essay questions and useful practice projects, you're well on your way to understanding a comprehensive and meaningful interpretation of *Pride and Prejudice*.

Q&A

1. Both Darcy and Elizabeth are guilty of exhibiting pride and prejudice throughout the novel. What are they proud of and what are they prejudiced against?

2. Mr. Bennet's estate is entailed. What does this mean?

3. How do Charlotte and Elizabeth differ in their views of marriage?

4. What reasons does Elizabeth give Darcy for turning down his first proposal?

5. Wickham claims that Darcy robbed him of a position as a clergyman. What really happened?

6. Where do Elizabeth's uncle and aunt Gardiner take her on their summer trip?

7. Why do Elizabeth and the Gardiner's have to cut their visit short?

8. Who is instrumental in finding Lydia and Wickham and in making sure Wickham married Lydia?

9. What encourages Bingley to ask Jane to marry him?

10. Who gives Darcy hope that Elizabeth may not turn down a second proposal?

Answers: (1) Darcy is proud of his social class and is prejudiced against the Bennet family's improper conduct and connections to the working class. Elizabeth's pride is wounded by Darcy's rejection of her at the first ball. She is prejudiced against Darcy's reserved and arrogant manners. (2) By law, the estate must be passed on to a male heir (Mr. Collins) upon Mr. Bennet's death. (3) Charlotte believes that women should marry for security, while Elizabeth believes they should marry for love.

(4) Elizabeth objects to Darcy's pride, his role in breaking up Bingley and Jane, and his treatment of Wickham. (5) Wickham traded the position for three thousand pounds. (6) Derbyshire county, where they visit Pemberley, Darcy's estate. (7) Lydia elopes with Wickham. (8) Darcy. (9) Darcy tells Bingley that Jane does have feelings for him. (10) Lady Catherine De Bourgh.

Identify the Quote: Find Each Quote in *Pride and Prejudice*

1. It is a truth universally acknowledged, that a single man in possession of a good fortune, must be in want of a wife.

2. Happiness in marriage is entirely a matter of chance. If the dispositions of the parties are ever so well known to each other, or ever so similar before-hand, it does not advance their felicity in the least.

3. I have been meditating on the very great pleasure which a pair of fine eyes in the face of a pretty woman can bestow.

4. But vanity, not love, has been my folly. Pleased with the preference of one, and offended by the neglect of the other, on the very beginning of our acquaintance, I have courted prepossession and ignorance, and driven reason away, where either were concerned. Till this moment, I never knew myself.

5. The upstart pretensions of a young woman without family, connections, or fortune. Is this to be endured! But it must not, shall not be. If you were sensible of your own good, you would not wish to quit the sphere, in which you have been brought up.

6. Ten thousand a year! Oh, Lord! What will become of me! I shall go distracted!

Answers: (1) Narrator. (2) Charlotte Lucas. (3) Darcy. (4) Elizabeth Bennet. (5) Lady Catherine De Bourgh. (6) Mrs. Bennet.

Essay Questions

1. Examine Austen's use of irony throughout the novel. Give examples of structural irony as well as irony within the narrator's descriptions and characters' dialogue.

2. Explore the developing relationship between Elizabeth and Mr. Darcy. How do they misunderstand each other, and when do they reach accord?

3. Why do you think *Pride and Prejudice* has such moving force for so many readers?

4. Darcy's behavior is very different at the end of the novel from what it is at the start. Do you think this change is credible within the story? Explain why or why not.

5. How do Elizabeth's forthrightness and independence represent an attack on the conservatism of characters like Lady Catherine De Bourgh?

6. The Meryton community is described as materialistic and fickle. How does town opinion affect the novel's progress?

7. Why is Elizabeth so anxious to distrust Mr. Darcy at the start of the novel, and to instead trust Mr. Wickham?

8. How do Elizabeth Bennet's ideas on marriage differ from her society's? Which characters in the novel share Elizabeth's views of marriage and which characters reflect society's perspective?

9. Show how Austen uses minor characters like Miss Bingley, Mr. Collins, and Lady Catherine De Bourgh to bring Elizabeth and Darcy together.

Practice Projects

1. Construct a Web site that could be used as a resource for other students reading *Pride and Prejudice*. The site could include a page about major themes in the book, a page about Jane Austen, and a page about the Regency period.

2. Write some journal entries from the perspective of one of the main characters.

3. Create a timeline that outlines the events of the novel.

4. Try doing a dramatic reading of the text, with different speakers reading the parts of the characters and narrator.

5. Before radio, television, or computers, people entertained themselves with music, dancing, and card games. Research one or more of these types of entertainment and present your findings to the class.

CliffsNotes Resource Center

The learning doesn't need to stop here. CliffsNotes Resource Center shows
you the best of the best—links to the best information in print and online
about the author and/or related works. And don't think that this is all we've
prepared for you; we've put all kinds of pertinent information at
www.cliffsnotes.com. Look for all the terrific resources at your
favorite bookstore or local library and on the Internet. When you're online,
make your first stop www.cliffsnotes.com where you'll find more
incredibly useful information about *Pride and Prejudice*.

Books

This CliffsNotes book, published by Wiley Publishing, Inc., provides a
meaningful interpretation of *Pride and Prejudice*. If you are looking for
information about the author and/or related works, check out these other
publications:

AUSTEN, JANE (Deidre Le Faye, ed.). *Jane Austen's Letters*. Oxford:
Oxford UP, 1997. A must-read for any Austen fan or scholar.
Austen's letters are witty and entertaining and give readers a strong
sense of her distinctive personality.

COPELAND, EDWARD, ed. *The Cambridge Companion to Jane Austen*.
Cambridge: Cambridge UP, 1997. A thorough critical introduction
to Austen and her works. Essays examine Austen's life and writing
from both a historical and contemporary perspective and also provide an excellent overview of the history of Austen criticism.

DAWKINS, JANE. *Letters from Pemberley, the First Year: A Continuation
of Jane Austen's Pride and Prejudice*. New York: Chicken Soup Press,
1999. The most recent and best reviewed of the sequels to *Pride and
Prejudice*. The book consists of a series of letters from Elizabeth to
Jane describing her new life as a wife and mistress of Pemberley, and
would be a worthwhile read for any lover of the original novel.

FOLSOM, MARCIA MCCLINTOCK, ed. *Approaches to Teaching Austen's
Pride and Prejudice*. New York: The Modern Language Association
of America, 1993. An excellent resource for teachers, students, and
general readers. Folsom discusses different editions of the novels,

criticism, and strategies for discussion. She then presents a series of essays that help readers to understand the novel's social history, structure and theme, and language.

MOLER, KENNETH L. *Pride and Prejudice: A Study in Artistic Economy.* New York: Twayne, 1989. Provides a thorough discussion of the novel. The author explains the importance of *Pride and Prejudice* and its critical reception. Additionally, the author gives the novel a careful reading and examines the various themes and motifs that occur throughout the book.

POOL, DANIEL. *What Jane Austen Ate and Charles Dickens Knew.* New York: Touchstone, 1993. An enjoyable book for anyone interested in learning more about the historical context of *Pride and Prejudice* or any other nineteenth-century British novel. It includes a wealth of information regarding aspects of daily life and also contains a useful glossary of terms commonly used during the period.

TOMALIN, CLAIRE. *Jane Austen: A Life.* New York: Vintage Books, 1997. A compelling biography that is well-researched and skillfully written. Tomlin details Austen's life in an engaging narrative style that will transport readers back to early-nineteenth-century England and make them eager to read all of Austen's works.

It's easy to find books published by Wiley Publishing, Inc. You'll find them in your favorite bookstores (on the Internet and at a store near you). We also have three web sites that you can use to read about all the books we publish:

- www.cliffsnotes.com

- www.dummies.com

- www.wiley.com

Video

A & E Presents Pride and Prejudice. 1996. A visually delightful adaptation of *Pride and Prejudice.* Purists may disagree with the minor changes made to characters and scenes to give the production a more modern and romanticized tone, but overall it is faithful to Austen's voice and vision. This film version is the perfect introduction of the story and period to students.

> *BBC Video Presents Pride and Prejudice.* 1979. An older, but accurate depiction of *Pride and Prejudice.* The sets are rather low-budget, but the cast and language are very close to the descriptions and dialogue in the novel.

Internet

Check out these Web resources for more information about *Pride and Prejudice* and Jane Austen:

Austen.com, `http://www.austen.com`—Provides extensive links to Austen-related sites, including full-text versions of Austen's books.

Jane Austen Concordance, `http://www.concordance.com/austen.htm`—A fantastic resource for anyone teaching or writing a paper about one of Austen's books. The electronic concordance allows you to type in the word or phrase you are looking for and it searches the entire text of the book for you.

The Regency Page, `http://locutus.ucr.edu/~cathy/reg.html`—A phenomenal collection of information and links about everything and anything you might need to know about the Regency period.

The Republic of Pemberley, `http://www.pemberley.com/`—A fun site to browse. It offers discussion groups on each of Austen's novels and links to other Austen sites. The highlight of this site, however, is the Jane Austen Information Page, which contains links to the complete texts of her novels and minor writings, annotations for her works, biographical information, and other miscellaneous materials such as "A Jane Austen Top 10 Song List."

The Victorian Web, `http://landow.stg.brown.edu/victorian/victov.html`—A phenomenal collection of information and links about everything and anything you might need to know about the Victorian era. Topics include history, religion, gender matters, technology, economics, and the visual arts, to name a few.

Next time you're on the Internet, don't forget to drop by `www.cliffsnotes.com`. We've created an online Resource Center that you can use today, tomorrow, and beyond.

Index